I Hope You Will All Remember Me

Nancy Catharine Albright Yow (1830-1919), dear wife of Matthew Christenberry Yow, and mother of Henry, Nancy, Mary Jane, Joseph, and John, their five little children (image courtesy of Larry R. Yow).

I Hope You Will All Remember Me

THE Civil War Letters OF
Matthew C. Yow
48th North Carolina Infantry

Nancy Yow Holt

Copyright © 2024 by Nancy Yow Holt

All rights reserved.

No part of this book may be reproduced in any form or by any electronic or mechanical means, including information storage and retrieval systems, without written permission from the author.

ISBN (hardback) 979-8-9897219-0-0

ISBN (paperback) 979-8-9897219-1-7

Library of Congress Control Number: 2023924091

Published in Jacksonville, Illinois.

Cover design by Burt&Burt / Photo of Matthew C. Yow and his letters courtesy of Larry R. Yow / North Anna Battlefield Park monument courtesy of Nancy Y. Holt / 1864 photo of canvas pontoon bridge across the North Anna by Timothy H. O'Sullivan, Library of Congress

For
Stephanie, Nicholas, Kathryn
and all the descendants of
Matthew Christenberry Yow
and
Nancy Catharine Albright Yow

Contents

Acknowledgments	ix
Preface	xi
Introduction	xv
Chapter One *April 20 – June 22, 1862*	1
Chapter Two *July 4 – November 30, 1862*	17
Chapter Three *January 18 – April 21, 1863*	33
Chapter Four *June 17 – August 30, 1863*	47
Chapter Five *September 10 – November 20, 1863*	75
Chapter Six *January 5 – April 4, 1864*	93
Chapter Seven *April, 1864 – April, 1865*	107
Appendix A *Remembrance and Reconciliation*	121
Appendix B *The Soldiers of Co. D of the 48th North Carolina Infantry*	125
Appendix C *Yow and Albright Family Trees*	145
Notes	151
Bibliography	177
Index	181

Acknowledgments

During visits to my grandmother's home in North Carolina as a child, I tagged along as my father and his brother searched for and found family stories. We walked through cemeteries and sifted through drawers to find clues from pictures, letters, and newspaper clippings. That experience set the stage for me when, fifty years later, I was shown a collection of Civil War letters written by Matthew C. Yow, my great-grandfather. The amateur genealogist inside of me responded with a desire to tell the story those letters contained. I was challenged because I did not know much about the war and had little writing experience other than college papers. I felt compelled to learn what I needed to so I could share the story of my great-grandparents. I am grateful to the people who helped and encouraged me to that end.

My cousin, Larry Yow, one of Matthew's great-grandchildren and the keeper of the letters, has shared so much about Matthew and his family with me. Larry is a first-rate Civil War history buff and family historian; conversing with him has been extremely helpful. In addition to giving permission to publish the letters, he has provided images to be used in the book. Larry's

Acknowledgments

wife, Glenda, a hospitable hostess, has welcomed me and other family members, with delicious food, iced tea, and good conversation. We have spent much time in their basement, more like a family museum, which has become one of my favorite places on the planet. Thanks to you both, Larry and Glenda.

I am thankful to the many good authors and historians (listed in the bibliography) who have helped me climb a steep learning curve. They have all been my teachers about the Civil War. Thanks to the staff at the Abraham Lincoln Presidential Library in Springfield, Illinois for assisting me with many volumes of books. Thanks to the staff of many Civil War places who provided answers to my questions.

To my friends who were curious if I would ever finish my writing project, thanks for inquiring about my progress. To my siblings – Mark, Carol, Matt, and Max, and their families – thanks for showing interest during my writing journey. Whether you scanned letters, read portions of the manuscript, provided images, or asked for an update, it is all appreciated. Special thanks to you, Carol, for encouraging me to "just finish the book" when I felt too challenged by the task.

To my children, thanks for your support. Stephanie, thanks to you and Patrick for gifting me with Civil War books. Nick, thanks for reading portions of the manuscript and giving valuable feedback. Kathryn, the oft-heard "Mom, how is your book coming along?" was a treasured encouragement to me. You are all dearly loved and I am happy to be publishing your great-great-grandfather's Civil War letters.

To my husband, Steve, thank you for helping me set up a new space to write in; having separate home offices probably made you as happy as it did me. Along life's way, thanks for being my companion at many places for many years, including most recently, Civil War battlefields and museums.

Preface

Matthew C. Yow, a North Carolina Confederate soldier, wrote home often during the American Civil War. The fifty-eight letters that make up this collection are addressed mostly to Catharine, his wife, and his dear little children. The remaining few addressed to his father, Catharine's father, and a few others, found their way to Catharine and so were preserved. Not all letters that Matthew wrote are part of this collection; some were undoubtedly lost in the Confederate mail system and some may have been distributed to others by Catharine or the subsequent letter keepers. What we have available gives us a good view into the lives of Matthew, Catharine, their children, their extended families, the people of Moore County, and the soldiers of the 48th North Carolina Infantry Regiment.

Catharine cherished the letters from Matthew and kept them safe during her lifetime. At the time of her death in 1919, she was living with her youngest son, John, and the letters were passed on to him. They were then passed down to Roland Yow, Matthew's grandson, and then again to the present keeper of the

Preface

letters, Larry Yow, a great-grandson of Matthew. A few years ago, Larry and this writer, a great-granddaughter of Matthew, discussed making the letters available to other descendants, something he had pondered for a while. They are now transcribed, researched, edited, and ready to be shared with those interested in Matthew's story, a common story of that time, about a husband with young children who reluctantly joined the Confederate army instead of being conscripted into service.

Matthew had fairly good handwriting which helped with the transcription process. Even so, there were portions that were difficult to read due to creasing, ink blots, and handling over time. By enlarging the text and adding contrast, some of the most difficult portions to read became legible. Matthew's random use of capital letters, lack of punctuation, missing words, inconsistent spelling, and incorrect grammar added to the challenge. It was decided that minimal editing would be done in order to preserve the charm and humor that is seen in his and many other letters of the period. To this end, Matthew's original spelling and grammar have been retained. As we read the letters we are able to "hear" Matthew the way the original recipients heard him. The addition of periods (but no other punctuation) and the application of capitalization rules allows for easier reading. Missing words that can be inferred based on Matthew's other letters and the context have been italicized and enclosed in parentheses. Dashes indicate content that is either missing or indecipherable.

These letters do not answer all the questions we have about Matthew's military service. Even so, they are a treasure trove for those who wish to know more about the hardships suffered by Civil War soldiers and their families. In these writings, we feel Matthew's pain of separation from Catharine and the children: the homesickness, the anxiety of going weeks without knowing how they were doing, and the frustration of being unable to provide for their needs. Matthew left his heart at home to go fight a rich man's war; his missives leave no doubt that his highest priority was his family – the wife and children he left behind in Moore County. His story compels us to empathize with the ordinary people, who were caught up and tossed about, by the turbulent winds of politics, social change, and war.

There is an endearing story that has come to us through the telling of family history. It is said that Catharine carried Matthew's most recent letter with her in her apron pocket; its presence gave comfort to her as she tried to get through each new day. Whether in the fields working or in the home cooking and caring for the children, she could pause and read the letter again or at least hold it close to her heart. Surely each letter was a source of hope until the next one arrived indicating that her husband was still in the land of the living, at least at the time he wrote and mailed it. As each new missive arrived the previous one found its resting place in the top drawer of an old mahogany dresser. Catharine's treasured bundle of correspondence from Matthew was her only tangible link to him in a world that was turned upside down by war.

One hundred and sixty years have passed since Matthew and Catharine shared their most intimate thoughts and feelings with each other on paper during the days of the Civil War. They and their generation are at peace now. Matthew's letters remain. His and Catharine's story is now shared for the first time with their many descendants and others who wish to know more about that terrible conflict from the perspective of an ordinary man and his family. This is not just Matthew and Catharine's story, though; it is the story of many families of the South during those days, a story of excessive hardship, fear, death, and hope. Matthew wanted to be remembered by those he loved most. In a

Preface

letter to his wife and children dated May 23, 1862, he wrote, "I hope you will all remember me." It is the desire of this great-granddaughter of Matthew and Catharine to see his hope extended to this generation.

— Nancy Yow Holt

Introduction

On the eighth day of March in 1828, in Moore County, North Carolina, Henry Yow and his wife, the former Nancy Elizabeth Jones, welcomed their first child; they named him Matthew Christenberry Yow. The 1850 United States census informs us that Matthew was one of eleven children. We also know from that year's census that he was a farmer, as were his father and grandfather before him. Matthew married Nancy Catharine Albright, the daughter of Joseph and Nancy Whitsitt Albright of Randolph County, in December of 1852. In 1860, according to the census, the young couple lived at dwelling number 686, near Robbins, within the postal area known as the Gold Region. The names of three little ones are clearly listed on the 1860 census by the hand of the enumerator: William Henry born in 1854, Nancy Elizabeth born in 1856, and Mary Jane born in 1858. Their fourth child, Joseph Gibbs, was born in 1860 after the census was taken. Little additional information is known about Matthew's life before the war. His mother, a member of the Methodist Episcopal Church, must have influenced Matthew with her devout ways as his letters reveal a man of faith.[1] We

Introduction

also know that he was involved with a fraternal organization that practiced charitable deeds. This we know from a newspaper notice in 1864, after his death, that described him as "ever ready and willing to discharge the duties of a Mason and soldier."[2]

Matthew and Catharine were grateful for their abundant blessings. They had prospered during the 1850s, as had most of the county's citizens,[3] and from the porch of their Piedmont home could view the fruits of their labor. In the fields grew corn, wheat, oats, potatoes, onions, beans, peas, carrots, and other subsistence crops. The young couple worked hard to make ends meet; they were part of the more than seventy percent of the state's population who did not own slaves.[4] Their livelihood as yeoman farmers provided them with all they needed for a good life. The excess that was grown or produced could be used to barter or pay for their additional needs and wants. Catharine's domestic chores kept her busy sewing clothes and preparing and preserving the food. There were also cows, horses, and hogs to care for. The children worked alongside their parents on the farm and in the home in age-appropriate ways. Henry, Nancy, and Jane were quite young but they could feed the animals, pick berries, and rock their baby brother, Joseph.[5] Life on the farm was a family affair where no one sat idle.

Despite the demands of farm life, the young family made time to enjoy community events, church meetings, and family gatherings. In 1860, wherever people congregated, the conversation usually turned to politics and the drama surrounding the upcoming presidential election. Most North Carolinians, especially the non-slaveholding farmers and Quakers, did not get caught up in the secession frenzy; for the most part, they wanted their state to stay in the Union.[6] When Abraham Lincoln won the election in November of that year, Matthew and the people of his state watched as South Carolina, Mississippi, Florida, Alabama, Georgia, Louisiana, and Texas left the Union one by

Introduction

one and by the first of February 1861, had formed the Confederate States of America. The governor, John W. Ellis, while leaning toward secession, knew that the state's citizens were cautious; they preferred to "watch and wait" to see what Lincoln's plan of action would be after his inauguration.[7] So cautious were they that the men of North Carolina voted on February 28, 1861, against a convention to consider secession as the next course of action.[8] North Carolina stayed in the Union. Life was happy, prosperous, and peaceful in this area of the Old North State, but the rumblings of war were growing louder. Life was about to change for Matthew and his family in unimaginable ways.

Spring arrived and with it came war when Confederate forces bombarded Fort Sumter on April 12, 1861. Three days later, when President Lincoln called for 75,000 troops to suppress the rebellion, Governor Ellis refused to provide his state's quota. More of the citizens were now in favor of secession because they did not want to be coerced by the politicians in Washington to fight against their neighbors in the seceded states. On May 20, 1861, an ordinance of secession was passed and North Carolina joined the Confederate States of America behind Virginia and Arkansas. Tennessee would soon join. The politicians had made their choices and now the people would become characters in the greatest calamity of their time.

Matthew did not respond to Governor Ellis' first call for troops in the spring of 1861. Many men of the state did, however, including two of Catharine's younger brothers – Henry, a 25-year-old constable, and John, a 22-year-old farmer, both single. Her older brother, William, who had a wife and four young children, chose not to enlist. The summer of 1861 ended with two good victories for the South, Big Bethel and First Manassas, but many soldiers were becoming dissatisfied with the war, and desertion rates increased. Volunteerism dwindled and

Introduction

the demand for troops could not be met. To remedy this the Confederate Congress passed the Conscription Act of 1862 which allowed the government to draft all eligible white males between 18 and 35 years of age into service for a three-year-term.

On February 28, 1862, Matthew enlisted for service in the Confederate army. He was going to turn 34 years old in March and decided to volunteer as opposed to being drafted. This would allow him to collect the fifty-dollar bounty and the opportunity to join a company with familiar people such as cousins and neighbors. During the five weeks between enlistment and reporting for duty, Matthew prepared Catharine for his departure by informing her about everything concerning the farm and home. Arrangements were made for one of Matthew's younger brothers, Jones, to live with Catharine and the children; she would need additional help on the farm in the coming months because she was five months pregnant. Matthew joined his Moore County comrades of Company D of the 48th North Carolina Infantry Regiment on the first Wednesday of April in Sanford, North Carolina at Buffalo Church. The people of the town prepared a lavish meal for the soldiers in the Masonic Hall and, afterward, there was preaching in the church sanctuary. The next morning, the men of the company thanked their hospitable hosts and "...took up the line of march for Raleigh."[9]

Matthew arrived with his company in the state capital within the first week of April and settled in with the rest of the regiment at Camp Mangum. The men were a motley crew ranging in age from seventeen to sixty-six.[10] They fit in well with the other soldiers of the regiment, "some being old men and some mere boys."[11] Although disparate in age, most of the men of the company were farmers.[12] The other companies were made up of recruits from the counties of Union, Davidson, Iredell, Chatham, and Forsyth. The elected officers for the regiment

Introduction

were Colonel Robert C. Hill,[13] Lieutenant Colonel Samuel H. Walkup,[14] and Major Benjamin R. Huske.[15] The troops were put on a strict schedule beginning with reveille at daybreak and ending with taps at 8:30 in the evening. Between those times they participated in squad, company, and battalion drills and an afternoon dress parade.[16] Matthew began writing home as soon as he could and made sure Catharine knew that he worked as hard every day at drilling as he did at home on the farm. After a month at Camp Mangum, the regiment relocated to Goldsboro where they continued drilling.

From Goldsboro, the regiment went by rail to Petersburg, Virginia. They arrived in the first part of June and set up camp at Dunn's Hill. They were attached to General Robert Ransom's brigade of Benjamin Huger's division.[17] During the next few weeks, Matthew and his comrades were involved in missions that included tearing up forty miles of the Norfolk and Petersburg Railroad. The first time the regiment came under enemy fire was during a mission in mid-June on the James River. No one died during the skirmish, but it was a reminder of the brevity of life and the seriousness of war. During the next few days, many regiments began to arrive in camp and Matthew wrote to Catharine that he anticipated "...a big battle before long." On the afternoon of June 25th, the regiment fought the enemy at French's Farm.[18] There, Matthew and his comrades advanced across an open field to fight Union troops sheltered in the woods behind a fence. This uneven match resulted in the loss of many men after which the regiment became known as "the Bloody 48th."[19] The regiment was detached from Ransom's brigade and after a few days of wandering, was attached to General John G. Walker's brigade. This was the extent of the unit's involvement in what became known as the Seven Days Battles which ended the Peninsula Campaign and drove General George B. McClellan's Army of the Potomac further from Richmond.

Introduction

By mid-July, Matthew and his regiment were back at Camp Lee in Petersburg where they remained for about six weeks. During this time, Matthew thought about the possibility of not making it back home. He had seen comrades fall by his side in battle and die of sickness in camp. He had his photograph taken and sent home to his family. He did not want to be forgotten. Catharine must have been thrilled to receive the "likeness" Matthew sent to her through a trusted relative. She now had an image to show the children when they talked about Papa. This would help them remember him.

On August 26th, Walker's brigade was sent by rail to Rapidan Station near Orange Court House. On the first of September, the troops left camp to go to Manassas but were too late to participate in the second battle there.[20] On September 4th, Southern troops began fording the Potomac River into Maryland. Matthew became ill possibly due to yellow fever and was sent to a hospital to recover. While he was away, the 48th participated in two important events: the surrender of Union forces at Harper's Ferry on September 15, 1862, to General Stonewall Jackson and two days later, the single bloodiest day of the war, the Battle of Antietam.[21] Had Matthew been with his regiment, he would have been exposed to some hard fighting near the Dunker Church where "...they were cut all to pieces."[22]

We know very little about Matthew's story from the time he became sick crossing the Potomac until the fifth of October when he wrote another letter to Catharine. What we do know from muster rolls is that Matthew deserted (most likely from the hospital) on September 7th and on October 4th was arrested and sent back to camp at Winchester.[23] He did not make it home at that time; we can only speculate about his adventures between the hospital and camp.

The regiment remained in Winchester until the 23rd of October. From there they traveled around and camped in

Introduction

various places. General Walker was transferred to the Western Theatre and John Rogers Cooke became brigadier general of a newly formed brigade consisting of the 15th, 27th, 46th, and 48th North Carolina regiments. This brigade was part of Ransom's division and Longstreet's First Corps. On the 22nd of November, they settled into camp around Fredericksburg. In his only letter home while encamped there, Matthew had the usual laments about the food but what he wrote about the troops' exposure to the weather was more serious than usual. There were many men in camp who were barefoot and there were no tents. Lt. Colonel Walkup wrote to Governor Vance[24] in October about the lack of supplies. In a heart-rending letter, he wrote about the "...suffering, exhausted, ragged, barefooted, and dying" as he shed light on the dire situation.[25] The troops were hungry, cold, and homesick. They were anticipating what we now know as the great Battle of Fredericksburg.

On December 13th, the 48th was in the "hottest of the battle."[26] At about 1:30 in the afternoon, they were ordered to occupy Willis Hill near Marye's Heights which exposed them to heavy artillery fire. They remained there until darkness to support their comrades crowded behind a stone wall along the Sunken Road. Down below, they could see thousands of Union troops charging over open ground and falling in defeat as the Confederates fired at them from behind the wall. The Union commander, General Ambrose E. Burnside, and his men finally retreated back across the Rappahannock River from whence they came, leaving their dead and wounded behind on a blood-soaked field. The 48th paid proportionately more for the Confederate victory compared to other regiments due to their position on the heights. Nineteen men were killed and 156 wounded.[27]

In early January 1863, the regiment arrived back in Petersburg. They were ordered along with the rest of Cooke's brigade

Introduction

to Pocotaligo, South Carolina, where they were involved with strengthening defenses along the coast. On April 22nd, they left Pocotaligo and returned to Wilmington, North Carolina, and then to Kinston where they went into camp.[28] On May 22nd, the brigade was sent into battle at Gum Swamp under General Daniel H. Hill to support the 56th North Carolina Regiment in a fight against a much larger enemy force.[29] They arrived in the late afternoon and assisted in driving back the Union army and afterward returned to Kinston. Cooke's brigade was now needed in Richmond and within a week would be on their way back to the Confederate capital.

Matthew was homesick. It had been 13 months since he last saw his wife and children. In his letters from the coast, he expressed hope that soon he would get a furlough. The day finally came and he was given 12 days from May 27th to June 7th to visit his family. He saw his youngest son, John Matthew, now 9 months old, for the first time. His three oldest children (Henry, Nancy, and Jane) probably ran to greet him and he scooped them all up at once. Little Joseph was only one year old when his father left for war; he may have been hesitant to run toward the scruffy-looking stranger. Matthew did not look like the Papa in the picture; it took a while before Joseph would sit on his Papa's lap again like old times. Catharine felt relief and gratitude for having her husband home again. Matthew visited with his family, friends, and neighbors and caught up on all the news. He saw for himself how the people in Moore County had changed and why Catharine had been pleading so much for him to come home. Moore and the surrounding counties including Randolph, Forsyth, Guilford, and Davidson were a hiding place for men who were dodging the draft or had deserted.[30] Some of these men banded together and caused grief and lawlessness in the community. There were also enemy raids. Catharine lived with the constant threat of harm to

Introduction

herself, the children, and the property. She felt safe with Matthew at home.

The days of the furlough ended and Matthew reluctantly left his family again. He boarded a train at the depot in High Point, North Carolina, and returned by June 7th to his regiment which was near Richmond. General Robert E. Lee was preparing to invade enemy territory again, this time in Pennsylvania, and Cooke's brigade would become part of Major General Henry Heth's division, in Lt. General A. P. Hill's Third Corps.[31] Matthew was on his way to Gettysburg as part of that campaign. Plans changed abruptly when Richmond was threatened and Cooke's brigade, among others, was ordered back to protect the capital. They were now doing fatigue and picket duties in the vicinity of Richmond while the majority of Lee's army in the Eastern Theatre was fighting the dreadful battle of Gettysburg during the first three days of July 1863. Cooke's brigade moved around for the remainder of the summer, repelling enemy forces around Fredericksburg and other areas close to the Confederate capital.

Near the end of September, the regiment relocated to Gordonsville. In early October, the troops were on the move again. On Wednesday, October 14th, a portion of General George G. Meade's Union army was traveling through Bristoe Station, when General A. P. Hill hastily, and without proper reconnaissance, ordered his two Tar Heel brigades into battle. The men of the two brigades advanced down a hill and into the open before they and the commanding officers realized they were badly outnumbered. The Confederates made a run for the railroad embankment and when almost there they realized the Union Second Corps soldiers were entrenched behind the tracks. Meade's soldiers opened fire, there was a bloody repulse, and the casualties were staggering. Matthew was hit but not hurt. Both of his brothers, Jones and Isaac, were wounded and sent home to recuperate. Both brigadier generals, Cooke and Kirkland, were wounded and out of service for months. This was the heaviest loss for the 48th North Carolina regiment thus far.[32]

Not long after this debacle, Lee began moving his army to the south side of the Rapidan River near Orange Court House. All thought that hostilities for the year had ended when on November 26th, Meade's army crossed the river to attack the Confederates. The offensive did not go well for the Federals; there was skirmishing but a major battle did not ensue since Lee's army was able to entrench near a stream called Mine Run. Meade's men recrossed the Rapidan less than a week later and the short campaign ended.

Matthew wrote to Catharine to inform her that the regiment had arrived at their winter quarters about three miles east of Orange Court House and built huts with chimneys in anticipation of a long and cold Virginia winter. Matthew and the men of the 48th were assigned to picket duty so he spent much of his time sitting in the cold under the stars reminiscing about the comforts of home. The men kept busy drilling and preparing for whatever battles the spring would bring. It was not all work though. Sometimes relatives and neighbors of the troops visited the camp; many came with baskets of food. There were opportunities for the soldiers to socialize with each other and the visitors. Matthew spent much of his free time doing so and writing letters, of course. Matthew, so homesick, wrote to Catharine and the children in one such letter dated January 27, 1864, "Lord, send that happy time when we shall meet again."

The fourth spring of the war arrived, and with it came anxiety. There was news in the camp that General Lee's army was going to be facing a much larger army led by the newly appointed general-in-chief of all Union armies, Ulysses S. Grant. He would make his headquarters with the Army of the

Introduction

Potomac led by General Meade. The next campaign of the long war would soon begin.

The following letters tell the story of Matthew, Catharine, their family members and neighbors, as well as the 48th North Carolina Infantry Regiment from April 1862 until April 1864. Matthew's story, after his last letter home, is told in the seventh chapter of this book.

April the 26: 1862 M C Yow

Dear wife and little children I now take my pen in hand to inform you that I am well with the exception of cold and caugh hoping when this comes to hand my find you all injoying the same blesing there are a greatdeal of sickness here several hav died and I am vary about you at home I hav riten five letters and no answer yet there must be somthing rong I want to here so bad I cant rest we got fifty dollars apeace and I want to send it to you if I can I donot want to keep it here tel the boys if they hav to come I want them to come to me but stay if you can if Jones does hav to come you must try to get some body to stay with you and the children I rote one letter to your father one to my father and one to W D Brower and two to you and no answer yet I can tel you I am not satisfied when I think of you and my childre my hart is ful for a soldires life is a hard one it is raining to day vary cold from the north east

This is the first page of the first letter that Matthew mailed from camp to Catharine and the children. It is dated April 26, 1862 (image courtesy of Larry R. Yow)

Chapter One
April 20 – June 22, 1862

"I must rite to you and the children for it may be the last time"

Matthew arrived at Camp Mangum near Raleigh early in April 1862 and started writing home as soon as he was settled. For Matthew, communication with his family and friends was the vital link between camp and home. In a letter to Catharine dated June 22, 1862, he wrote, "I want you to rite to me as often as you can and I will do the same."

Matthew adapted quickly to the salutations that were commonplace among the soldiers. He would start each letter with phrases such as "I now sit down to rite you a few lines..." or "I now take my pen in hand..." The quality of the composition of the letters evolved over time. In an early letter to Catharine, he interjected with apparent frustration, "I cant rite like I could talk" between unrelated thoughts. As time went on, his correspondence became smoother. Matthew also closed some letters according to the customs at that time with the phrase, "When this you see remember me tho many miles apart we be" or some slightly jumbled variation. Many of the letters closed with a plea for God's blessing on the recipient and a reminder that they were not forgotten.

Matthew had a list of people he wanted to hear from and to whom he would write to remind them of that. First and foremost were Catharine and the children. Also on the list were his father, father-in-law, and brothers. Some messages were given in letters to be passed on to mothers in the neighborhood about their sons such as the sad news that they were in the hospital or had been taken captive by the Yankees. In a letter dated April 26, 1862, shortly after arriving at camp, Matthew wrote to Catharine, "Give my best respects to all inquiring friends." Matthew wanted people back home to know he remembered them.

Matthew's reasons for writing home were many. Most importantly, he was interested in knowing how his family was doing health wise and keeping them updated about his wellbeing. There were ongoing conversations about toothaches, infections, sore throats, doctor visits, and even how to survive smallpox should the children contract it. Matthew also inquired often about the farm. He wanted to know what the weather was like, the amount of rainfall, the condition of the crops, and who was available to help Catharine with the hard work. Letters to people other than Catharine were written so as to invoke help for his family so their needs would be met.

Another reason for letter writing was to share the news and gossip. Matthew wrote details to Catharine about camp life, sermons, food, and battles, as well as the health and activities of her relatives and neighbors in the army. He in return wanted to know all the news about his household from the mundane to the important. Matthew also wanted to know about the political climate in Moore County and the activities of the outliers,[1] deserters, and unruly neighbors. There was also gossip to hope-

Chapter One

fully unravel through the mail such as Matthew's brother's relationship with Catharine's sister, Youtha. Matthew was always anxious to hear the latest hometown news.

The Confederate Postal Department was not dependable.[2] In order to save ten cents on postage and be more assured of delivery, Matthew often used the services of fellow comrades going on furlough, and visitors in camp to take letters home for him. It is probable that this method of delivering the mail was used more often than the postal service.[3] This system worked well for sending bulky or valuable gifts such as his likeness, money, sugar, soda, and items for the children. Matthew did send a special hand-carved ring to Catharine in a letter dated March 24, 1863, with the promise to send rings to Nancy and Mary Jane if she received it. It is not known if Catharine received the ring or not since the letter it was mailed in is not part of this collection. However, it is known that the girls received their rings later, the proof being that the one to Nancy was passed down to this writer.

Matthew devised a plan to determine which mail system was faster by sending a letter to Catharine on April 21, 1863, and another letter via his cousin, David Yow. He wrote to Catharine, "I thought I wold rite this morning and see which wold get home first David or the letter." Matthew was consistent about putting the date on letters he sent out. When writing to Catharine, he would often confirm receipt of her most recent letter with the date she wrote it and the date it was received. He noticed trends and wrote about various reasons for mail interruptions such as changing camps. It is interesting that much of what Matthew wrote about was the logistics of letter writing!

Matthew was an affectionate husband, father, brother, and son and it showed in the letters he wrote home. Because he was sentimental, Matthew did not hide his emotions; he never shied away from sharing his most heartfelt thoughts. In the book *The*

Life of Johnny Reb by Bell I. Wiley, Matthew and his comrades come to life. They were crude and tough at times but "...for the most part, men of warm affection and susceptible to the tenderest of emotions."[4] Matthew's letters demonstrate his warm affection and tenderness.

∼

April the 20: 1862   M C Yow

Deer Father Mother and Family[5]

 I now sit down to rite you a few lines to let you no ware I am at this time. I am at Camp Mangum.[6] I am well at this time hoping when this comes to hand may find you enjoying the same blesing. I could (*not*) get any man in my plase[7] so I had to go. I cannot when I can come home. Our colonel is vary tight on us. I am in the 48 regiment NC state troops under Colonel Hill.[8] I hav not hear from home since I left. I hav rote 3 letters and no answer yet. I want to here vary bad from you all. There are a great deal of sicknes in this camp and the worst caugh I ever herd. We have moved out about a mile from our old camp. I do not no how long we will stay here. We hav not got our money yet. We think we will get it soon. I want you to go and see my wife and little children when you can. Catharine is troubeld bad when I left. When I think of her (*and*) the children it fils my hart with greaf for I love them. Well I rote a few lines to Henry[9] and John[10] but hav got no answer yet. Our regiment is rite on the railrode now. I have bin to Raileigh once since I come to Camp Mangum. We here that the men from 18 to 35 had to inlist.[11] If this be so it will be a bad chanc at home. We have plenty to eat. We hav bacon beef sugar rice flour no corn. I want corn bread. We get soap and candles but I am not satisfied at all. Camp life is a hard and troublesome life to me. We are learning to drill vary

Chapter One

fast. I want to come home at harvest if I can but donot no how it will be. If I donot come I hope my friends will save my wheat and oats. I hav drawn one suit clothes one blanket two caps one canteen one haversack and one pare of shoes. I want you to soon direct your letters to Camp Mangum in care of Capt Clagg.[12] You must (*not*) look (*at*) my bad hand (*writing*). If I never see you no more on earth I hav a good hope that I may meet you all in heven. When this you see remember me tho fare apart we be so fairwill.

Matthew C. Yow

∽

April the 26: 1862   M C Yow

Deer Wife and Little Children

I now take my pen in hand to inform you that I am well with the exception of cold and caugh hoping when this comes to hand my find you all injoying the same blesing. There are a great deal of sicknes here. Several hav died and I am vary (*uneasy*) about you at home. I hav riten five letters and no answer yet. There must be somthing rong. I want to here so bad I cant rest. We got fifty dollars[13] appease and I want to send it to you if I can. I donot want to keep it here. Tel the boys[14] if they hav to come I want them to come to me but stay if you can. If Jones does hav to come you must try to get some body to stay with you and the children. I rote one letter to your father one to my father and one to W N Brower[15] and two to you and no answer yet. I can tel you I am not satisfied when I think of you and my children. My hart is ful for a soldires life is a hard one. It is raining to day vary cold from the north east. I must tel you that I work as hard evry day as I would at home. Drilling is hard work you may be sure. We hav to run the double quick. That is vary hard. We hav bacon beef flour sugar but we want something elce but we cant get anything with out paying double the worth. Egg are 20 to 25 cents. Chickens 50 cents each. I cant eate them. Pies 20 to 25 cents. I hav bin to Raleigh one time. I want to go again and get my likenes[16] taken and send it to you if I can. I cannot tel you when I can come home. I want to come about the tenth of June if I can. If I dont come you must do the best you can. I want you to tel me how you are geting along with your crop. When you rite direct your letter to Camp Mangum near Raleigh in cear of Capt Clagg the 48 regiment NC troops. Give my best respect to all inquiring friends. I want to here from you all. If you need any moore corn you buy it. So I must close. When this you see remember me tho many miles apart we be so fairwell to you all.

M C Yow

Golds Boro May the 17 1862

Deer Brother[17]

 I take my pen in (*hand*) to inform you that I am well with the exception a risen[18] in my yer which makes my head ach hoping when this comes to hand it may find you injoying the same great blesing. I receivd your kind letter to day. It giv me great satisfaction to here from you that you was geting along with your work so well. Jones when you rite to me rite with ink. I could hardly reed your letter it had rubd out so bad.

 Deer brother you said you had not drank any spirits sinc I left. I was glad to here that for I hav seen trouble about you. I hope the good Lord will bles and save you forever. I am looking for a letter from father. I hav rote to him and no answer yet. I want you all to rite. I want you to rite me when you get this. I hav bin vary uneasy about you. I was afraid you would hav to come

Chapter One

to the war. I want you to stay if you can. Dont come as long as you can stay. I want you to rite to me what the people say about coming. Several hav come to our company now and if you hav to come I want you to come to me. Jones take good (*care*) of my little children. Poor little children I want to see them so bad. I rote a letter to Isaac.[19] I suppose he has got it. William Pool[20] is well and as wicked as ever. He says he wants to see you all. A J Stuts[21] is well also. David D Yow[22] is sick. I must close my letter by saying may the good Lord bles and save us all for ever.

Your affectionate brother M C Yow so fairwell Simeon J Yow

Golds Boro N C May the 23 1862

Deer Wife and Little Children

I now take my pen in hand to let you no that I am well at this time hoping when this comes to hand it may find you all injoying the same great blesing. I must tel you that we hav to leav here tomarrow to go to Weldon stil futher from home but I hope the good Lord will be with me there. I want you to pray for me. I expect we shal hav to fight before long. Catharine do the best you can. I hope and pray we will meet again but if we dont I hope we will in haven whare we will part no more. Catharine try to rais the little children to love the Lord who can save them forever. Lord bless my little children.

Catharine when I think about the day we parted it fils my hart with sorrow. I do want to see you the worst I ever did. I cant rite like I could talk if I could see you. I rote to you and Jones. I hope you will get them. I rote father a letter yesterday. Catharine I saw your brothers. They ware both well. I was vary glad to see them. I must tel you that there is a greateal of sicknes here. Some die every day.[23] David D Yow is sick and I think he will get off.[24]

I Hope You Will All Remember Me

I expect to send this letter by him if he comes. Catharine I will rite as soon as I get to Weldon if I can and tel you no wher to rite. I will come home as soon as I can if I live but I cant tel you when that will be. Catharine and little children fairwell if I never see you any more.

Catharine if get in a battle and get kild I dont want you to greev about me. I hope I shal be prepard. I will rite as soon as I can when I get to Weldon. I have bin looking for letters from some of you. I rite vary often. I am glad to here that you are geting along so well with your work. William Henry my deer little son you said you wanted to rite me a letter. I wish you could. Henry you must be a good boy and help your mother and dont fight your little sisters. I want to see you all so bad but I cant see you soon. Catharine take good cear of what you hav got. I cant tel when I can help you any more. I want you to get what you need Catharine. I am riting and in trouble you may be sure. Catharine I thought I would get my likenes taken but I hav not yet. I will as soon as I can. You said you went with Jones to your fathers. I am glad you went. Go when you can leav.

Jones deer brother do the best you can for my wife and children and you shant loose nothing if I live. Jones I hope you will not hav leav home. If you do rite to me and I want you to come to me but stay if you can. Jones we parted in tears but I hope we will meet again. So fairwell brother.

Catharine another word to you and the children if (I) nevere see you no more I hope you will all remember me.

Nancy C Yow
William Henry Yow
Nancy E Yow
Mary J Yow
Joseph G Yow
Fairwell to you all
M C Yow N C Yow

Chapter One

Catharine I will send this letter (*by*) David D Yow. I hav too shilling of silver I will send by him. I receivd a few lines from Peter Moody.[25] He said you was all well. Tel him I will rite as soon as I can. I said we was going to Weldon but I dont no where we shal go. We shal leav in the morning the 24 of May. I must close. I hav not forgoten you yet. So fairwell.

             Matthew C. Yow

∼

M C Yow Mrs N C Yow
Peters burg VA June the 8 1862

Deer Wife and Little Children

I one more time take my pen to rite to you. I am well this blesed Sabbath morning. I hope when this comes to hand it will (*find*) you injoying the same great blesing. We hav just got back from our jurney. We left our camp Friday morning to meet the Yankies. We went about 40 miles towards Norfolk but we did not see them. Then we commenct tearing up the rail rode. We turnd it over about 15 miles. It was the best railrode I ever saw. It is the Norfolk and Petersburg rode.[26] It belongs to the Yankies. It rained all day Friday and rained Saturday evning again. There is the most rain I ever saw. It dont look like there will be anything made here. All the wheet I see is red with rust and thers not much wheet here.

Catharine if it rains as much up there as it does here it will be a bad chanc about your work but you must do the best you can and be saving for there will be hard times I am afraid. Take good cear of your salt[27] and do the best you can for I cant tel you when I can come home. I am afraid not soon if ever. Catharine I do want to see you and the children so bad. I do hope and pray that we will meet again before long. I dont no what hour we shal be cald to the battle field. The cannons was herd here yesterday supposed to be at Richmond. If hav to go I hope the good Lord will be with me there. Catharine I dont want you to greav so much about me. I no you are in trouble but bare it the best you can and pray to the Lord for my protection.

Catharine there will be no chanc for me to come home at harvest. You must get your wheet savd if you can. It seems like there is no chanc of peac til we shal all perish. I think thats what will end the war. For there is not much a making. There is hundreds of acres here lying idol and what is planted is always coverd in water.

Catharine I rote you a letter sinc I came here the 3 and one to Father the 4. I hope you hav got them.[28] I am looking for letters from you but we mov so much I am afraid I shal not get them all. I want you to rite when you get this. It may be that I will get your letters. Direct to M C Yow Co. D 48 regiment N C Troops General Ransoms Brigade Peters Burg Va.

Simeon J Yow deer brother I hav bin looking for a letter from you. I want to here from you how you are geting along with your crop. Jones you must do the best you can. I cant come to help you any. I do want to come to come home and help you cut wheet so bad. Jones try to save all the wheet you can. Deer brother fairwell

M C Yow

Catharine deer wife I must close my letter and I dont no what to say to you. My hart is ful. This may be my fairwell letter. If I never see you on earth I hope we will meet in haven where we shal part no more. Catharine try to rais my poor little children the best you can. Henry you must be a good boy.

Nancy E Yow   Mary J Yow

Joseph G Yow fairwell to you all.

Nancy C Yow deer wife fairwell.

Matthew C Yow your affectionate husband   rite soon

Chapter One

Simeon J Yow
Peters Burg Dinwiddie County VA
June the 11 1862

Deer Brother

I one time more sit down to drop you a few lines to let you no that I am well at present hoping when this comes to hand it may find you injoying the same great blesing. I receivd your kind letter the 10 which giv me great satisfaction to here that you was all well and geting along so well with your work. I am so glad to here that you are trying so hard to make somthing to liv on. It will be needed. Jones father says you work hard. I no I want to be with you. I red your letter and cride all the time. I am riting with tears in my eys. Work on brother and do the best you can. I am praying that we may meet again. I hop and trust my prares will be answered.

I believ you are all praying for me and I hop your prares will be answerd. I am afraid I cant come home soon. I am trying to get to come. I seems like there is no chanc to get a furlow but I hop that times will alter soon. I could (hear) the cannons roaring yesterday evning. I cant tel how long we shal stay here. We all want to come back to NC again for we dont get as much to eat here as we did there. We have drawd some now.

William Pool says he will rite you a letter today. He is as wicked as ever. A J Stuts is well. Jones deer brother I hav prayd for you and I hop you will quit all of your wicked ways and try to serv the Lord for the time to come. Tel Isaac to rite to me. I rote to him and I got no answer. I must close by saying may the Lord bles and sav us all for ever. fairwell

Matthew C Yow

I Hope You Will All Remember Me

~

June the 16 1862[29]
Direct your letter thus to M C Yow
Co D 48th regiment N C Troops General Ransoms
Brigade Petersburg VA

John said that Henry[30] got a letter from you last Friday. It is said by some that we shal leav here to day but I cant tel. We hav so many orders that we dont no one hour what we will do next. We hav got orders to leav now in a few minuts but I dont (*know*) were.

~

June the 19 1862   M C Yow
Petersburg Dinwiddie County VA

Deer Wife and Little Children

By the kind hand of Providenc I sit down to rite you a few lines to let you no that I am well at present hoping when this comes to hand it may find you injoying the same great blesing. On Monday the 16 we got orders to march. We marht about 12 miles to City Point and took up camp at dark. Co D with 3 other companys was orderd down to the river on picket which we did and stayd nearly all night. We could here the Yankie pickets hollow all night. We went back to our camp and eat our crackers and broild beef for our brakefast then we was orderd to march down to the river to attact[31] the Yankies which we did. We had 2 peaces of artlery. Tha fired on the gun boats and fired about 2 hours and tha commenct sheling of us so hard that our major[32] orderd us to retreat which we did in double quick time. The shels was bursting all around us but

Chapter One

nobody was hurt vary bad. I was sorter scard when tha fel so fast.

We got back to our camp the 18 all tired and hungry. I expect we shal hav to go back before long and try them again. Catharine I cant tel you all this time your brother John come to see me last Sunday. He was well. I want to go to see them if I can. Catharine I hav bin looking for a letter from you. I want to be at home so bad now to see you all and help you save the wheat and eat peas and unions but I cant come yet. I hav to stay here in trouble but I do hope and pray that I will get home to see you and the deer little children again. I believ you are praying for me and I hope your prares will be herd. Catharine dont greav so much about me for I do hope and pray that I will come to you again. I want you to rite soon and let me no how you are geting along with the wheat and oats. I will rite evry chanc I get. I want to here from you every day if I could. I rote your father a letter the 15. I must close for this time.

When this you see remembr me tho often times I think of you.

M C Yow
N C Yow

Petersburg Dinwiddie County June the 22 1862

Deer Wife and Little Children

By the kind hand of Providenc I one more time take my pen in hand to inform you that I am well at present hoping when this comes to hand it may find you all injoying the same great blesing. I receivd your kind letter the 21 which giv me great satisfaction to here from you all again and to here that you was all well but I was sorrow to here that the wheet was so sorry. I am afraid you will not hav enough for bread but you must take good cear of it and do the best you can for I hope and pray to the Lord that I will get home again to see you and my poor little children. I want to see you all so bad it seems like I cant bare it. I red your letter and tears dropt from my eyes all the time. Catharine I expect we shal hav another battle before long for the last week there has come 6 or 7 regiments here from NC and tha keep coming. The 26 has just come this morning. That is the one Columbus Harrison[33] is in but I hav not bin to them.

Catharine I expect we shal hav to leav here before long. We are orderd to cook three days rations and I no we will hav to leav. I expect there will be a big battle before long and I hop that will end the war. If it dont stop before long we shal all suffer at home and in the army. Catharine I told you not to greav but you say you cant help it. I no you cant for I am in as much trouble as any body ever was but I put my trust in the good Lord. Catharine I hav prayd all the time that I might be savd and get home to my wife and poor little children. For I do want to see them so bad I dont no what to do. Catharine I believ you are praying for me. Deer wife pray on and if I never see you on earth any more I hope we will meet in haven where we will part no more. Catharine I shed tears of greaf evry day. Matthew C Yow Nancy C Yow

Catharine I dont no what to rite for I am in a greateal of trouble about you and the poor little children for I am afraid I never shal see you all again. I am riting today. It is the Sabbath. I got fathers letter when I got yours. I want to rite to you both today if I can. I must stop and go to preaching. We hav preaching evry Sunday.[34] I hav bin to preaching and I will try to rite some more. Catharine tel old granfather[35] that I want to see him mity bad. I am glad to here that he is well and that he is praying for me. I hope and pray to the Lord that his prares will be answerd and tell Nancy[36] that Columbus is here now and is well. I expect

Chapter One

we will all hav to fight to gether. It is hard to think of but I will put my trust in the good (*Lord*).

Catharine I rote you a letter about our battle on James River but let that not scear you. But we was all in a close place. The shels was bursting all over us like thunder but we all escapt unhurt but I cant tel how it will be next time. I thought I would go and see Henry and John today but I cant go today. I must rite to you and the children for it may be the last time but I hope not. I want you to rite to me as often as you can and I will do the same.

Jones I want you to stay at home if there is any chanc for I dont want you to come to this bad plase. Do the best you can. I hope I shal come to see you all again. Jones I am in trouble but I put my trust in the Lord. I read your letters and cry all the time. Rite soon and fail not. I was glad to here that you was geting along so well with your crop. I remain your brother until death So fairwell. M C Yow S J Yow

Catharine I must say a word to you and my deer little children. Deer wife continue your prares for me. You may be sure I hav not forgoten you. William Henry be a good boy. May the Lord bles the children. I must close. My hart is ful so fairwell deer wife and children Nancy C Yow.

Matthew C Yow

Catharine i want you to get leather and hav shoes made for you and the children i want them to hav shoes henrey must hav shoes i want you to rite to me all about your things your hogs and cattle and how much Corn you made i want to no if you are out of bacon yet and how much meat you can mak this fall you must do the best you can and be saving for the hard times has not come yet i dont no what you will do for salt you and father must try to get some if you can Catharine i will rite Again as soon as i can and tel you more than i can now
       Nancy C yow
William henry my dear little son you must be a good boy and help your mother and read your book Lord bless the dear children

This is the third page of a letter to Catharine and the children dated October 28, 1862. This letter shows Matthew's many concerns about his family. He wanted to know the details about the hogs, cows, corn, and other aspects of the farm. Matthew worried about Catharine's ability to handle the extra workload in his absence. He knew that Catharine had many decisions to make such as when to make beef of the cow. Matthew could not help her but he encouraged her with the oft-repeated words "do the best you can" (image courtesy of Larry R. Yow).

Chapter Two
July 4 – November 30, 1862

"Do the best you can"

Matthew and Catharine needed more than just the exchange of information during the long days of the Civil War. Their correspondence with each other also provided much needed encouragement. Matthew, knowing that his wife was overwhelmed with responsibilities, tried to manage the farm and handle domestic affairs by giving advice through the mail. He often encouraged her with the words, "Do the best you can." Jones, Matthew's brother, would soon be enlisted into the army and would not be able to continue helping his sister-in-law with the duties on the home front. This timing, during the summer of 1862, was not good because Catharine was expecting her fifth child.

The news traveling back and forth via letters brought a mix of emotions to both writers. Matthew was relieved to hear that the wheat was all cut and in the barn. Catharine was troubled by the description of the battle that occurred on the 25th of June. Good news or bad news could be dealt with as it came but no news brought added anxiety. Such was the case for a period of two months between early August to mid-October when Catharine did not receive any letters from Matthew and, for a portion of that time, Matthew was unable to receive Catharine's letters. Unbeknownst to Catharine, Matthew was trying to get home. Unfortunately, he did not succeed in his travels; he was arrested and sent back to camp.

Catharine gave birth to a healthy baby boy on August 28th; she tentatively named him Matthew. He was the third son and according to a popular naming pattern at the time, would be named after his father.[1] The two older boys were named Henry and Joseph according to this pattern that named the first son after the paternal grandfather and the second son after the maternal grandfather. We can presume that their daughters were named according to this pattern since the speculation fits; Nancy may have been named after her maternal grandmother (which was her paternal grandmother's name also), and Jane was possibly named after Catharine's sister who died the year she and Matthew were married. Catharine was doing the best she could with all of life's duties, but she chose to wait for Matthew's agreement before making a final decision on the baby's name.

Weeks passed and Catharine did not hear from her husband. She was without a doubt encouraged anew when she received a letter dated October 5, 1862, in which Matthew declared, "I no you think I am dead but thank the Lord I am alive yet." The letter writing resumed and each caught the other up with events concerning the battle and home fronts, including naming the new baby. Matthew wrote exactly two months after his birth, "If it wold suit you John Matthew."

Matthew and the other soldiers encouraged their wives so often with the words, "Do the best you can" that it "...became a widespread cliché, its very usage suggesting the commonality of the experience."[2] The absent husbands encouraged their wives

Chapter Two

with this phrase knowing that they could not always give detailed advice since they did not know all the circumstances at home. As much as he could, Matthew made domestic decisions from afar, but when he couldn't he had confidence in Catharine's judgment and therefore he could say to her, "Do the best you can."

∽

July the 4 1862
Petersburg VA M C Yow

Deer Wife and Little Children

By the kind hand of Providenc I take my pen in hand to rite you a few lines to let you no that I am well and unhurt yet and I do hope these lines may find you injoying the same great blesing. I receivd your kind letter to day. It giv me great plesure to here from you all one time more. I must tel you about my travels for the last ten days. We left Petersburg the 24 and went to Richmond and Wensday the 25 we went into the battle field[3] and about one hour by sun in the evning we had a hard battle. We had five hundred men and we fought five thousand 25 minuts when we was orderd to retreat and then the Georgians[4] came in and help us and we drove them back. We lost one hundred and four of our regiment kild and wonded 20 kild and 84 wonded. A J Stuts got his leg broke by a ball and it had to be cut off. Isaac Brady[5] was kild dead on the field.

Our captain[6] was badly wonded in the thigh and Lieutenant Anderson[7] was wonded in leg. Major Husk[8] wonded in the foot. I can tel you it was an awful sight. We kild a heep of the Yankies. I (saw) some of them lying on the field on Friday after the battle. I shot 6 times at them with good aim. I expect I kild some body and I dont want to fight any more. That was enough for me. I suppose we hav taken 100 pecies of artilary in the 8 days fiting and we hav whipt them all out from there and I dont no were tha will try next. We hav evry place ful of prisnors. We (*have*) 25 or 30 thousand. Some of them come and giv them selvs up. Some thinks tha wont fight much more. I hope tha will not. Catharine I no you think I am ded for I haint had no chanc to rite tel now. I got fathers letter to day and all them you sent. Your brothers is both alive and well. John was here when I was reding your letter. He said he rote you a letter. He said he was nock dow by a bom shel.

    Catharine you said tha had savd all the wheet and you must pay the hands for there work. I was glad to here that the grain was all cut and in the barn. I red all of the letters and shed many tears. I was seting studing about you and the pore little children when the letters come and I was so glad that (*I*) sat rite (*up*) and red them and cried all the time. I no you are in trouble about me for I hav not (*written*) in many days but dont be troubled for I (*am*) alive and I thank the Lord for it. For I hav bin praying all the time for the Lord to sav me that I might get home to my wife and blesed little children again and I hope our prares hav (*been*) herd and answerd. Tel my poor old granfather that I hav not forgoten him yet. I want to see him mity bad. Tel him to pray for me. I do hope and pray to the Lord that I shal see you all again in this world. I hope we will get back to NC again before long I hope. I hope that times will get better and I can get to come home to see you all again. Catharine tel father that I will rite to him before long. We are not at Petersburg now. we are about 11 miles from there on the rode a resting. I think we will go back to our camp before long. Send your letters to Petersburg VA General Walkers[9] Brigade Co D 48 regiment NC Troops. We joind another brigade. Colonel Hill and General Ransom fel out and he left him.[10]

    Jones I will rite to you before long when I get back to the

Chapter Two

camp and if you hav to come I want you to come to me. Tel Isaac the same but stay if you can. So deer brother fairwell. M C Yow. John Williamson[11] says he wants his people to rite to him.

 Catharine my deer wife I must a word to you. Continue your prars for me I am praying all the time. Lord save us all I pray. We hav to march now. So fairwell deer wife and little children.

Matthew C Yow Nancy C Yow

Petersburg VA July the 10:1862
M C Yow Nancy C Yow

Dear Wife and Dear Little Children

 I one time more take my pen in hand to rite you a few lines to let you no that I am well at present and unhurt and I do hope when this comes to hand it may find you all in good helth. I receivd your letters of the 28 the 4 of July and I no that you hav sent me a letter but I hav not got it yet. I expect tha hav gon to Ransoms brigade and I am afraid that I will not get them. We belong to Walkers brigade now. we are at our camp at Petersburg. I want to here from you all vary bad. we hav to pay ten cents on a letter now but I rite as long as I can get any money. I am scears of money now. I think we shal get some money before long. I want you to rite as often as you can. I will send you some stamps if I can to mail letters.

 Catharine I no you was uneasy about me but I went through safe thank the Lord. I praid for the Lord to save me and I hope my prares was herd. The balls came as thick as hail around me but none of them hit me. I no you hav red about the battle. The line of battle is said to be 15 miles long. I wish you could see what I hav seen. It is awful to think of to see dead men lying all over the ground not buried and a great many of them was never buried at all. I saw some that had bin dead 2 days. the same ones we kild. I must (*tell*) you that Capt Clegg is dead.[12] James Dowd[13] will be our capt now. I do hop and pray that the war will soon close so I can come home to see you all again. I do want to see you all so bad. It fils my hart when I try to rite to rite to you but I hop the good Lord will be with me to the end. Catharine your brothers come out safe. John said he rote you a letter before the battle. A J Stuts was wonded and he is at Richmond in the hospital. His leg was cut of. I am mity sorrow for him.

Catharine I am afraid that Jones will hav to leav you. I hav herd that the conscript will hav to come the 15 of this month. I do hope he will not. I dont think tha can mak them come. If I was there I wold try them a while.

Any how Jones stay if you can for I want you to stay with my wife and little children tel I come back. Jones I believ you are good to them and will tak cear of them. I do want to come home so bad to get somthing to eat. I want beans and potatoes and milk and butter. we cant get these things here. Butter is one dollar a pound. Tobacco 5 cents a plug. Milk 10 cents a quart. Catharine I want you to rite to me all about your things how tha are geting along. You dont no how bad I want to see you. I do hope and pray that I can com home again to see you and the blesed little children. It seems like I could take them all in my arms at one time. Lord bles and save my dear wife and little children. May the good Lord bles and sav us all for ever is my prare. Direct your letters to Petersburg VA General Walkers Brigade 48 regiment NC Troops Co D in cear of Capt Dowd.

Catharine do the best you can and be saving with what you hav got. Take good (*care*) of your wheet. Dont sell none of the wheet if you can help it. Keep it for bread. I do hope I can come home before long. Some says the last battle is fought and I think tha will giv furlows after a while. Tha wont giv none now. Catharine giv my best respect to all of my friends and relations.

Chapter Two

Tel father to rite when he can for it revivs me when I get your letters. Tel old granfather that I hav not forgoten him yet. Tel him to pray for me. Catharine I must close for this time. Pray for me and I hope and believ your prares will be answerd. May the Lord bles and save us all. So fairwell for this time Nancy C Yow.

M C Yow

~

Nancy C Yow August the 4 1862
Petersburg VA Camp Lee M C Yow

Dear Wife and Little Children

I one more time take my pen in hand to rite you a few lines to let you no that I am well at this time hoping when this comes to hand it may find you all in good helth. Catharine I will tel you what I am going to do. I am going to send my likenes[14] to you by Lewis Maness[15] and I will send you some money. I will send you 60 dollars now and you can keep it tel you need it and I will send you some more invelops. He said he wold take all to you and I know he will do what he says. I haint got time to rite much this tim. I will rite before long again.

Catharine you sent me some butter and I was glad to get it. I cold sold it for one dollar a pound if I wold. Butter sels here for one dollar a pound and unions ten cents a peac. I cold hav sold them that John sent me at 20 cents a peac. Apples sel for 15 and 25 cents a dosen but I dont buy them. I hire my washing don and I hav to pay 10 to 15 cents for a shirt and not half washt at that. I got them washt at Goldsboro for 5 cents. Catharine my loving wife I must close for this time. May the good Lord bles and sav you is my prare.

Catharine I want you to rite as often as you can. Catharine

my dear wife do the best you can. May the Lord bles and sav you and my blesed little children forever is my prare.

Matthew C Yow to his dear Wife Nancy C Yow So fairwell for this time.

∼

Petersburg VA Camp Lee
August the 6: 1862

Deare Wife and Little Children

I now tak my pen in hand to rite you a few lines to let you no that I am well at this time and I do hop when this comes to hand it find you all well. Catharine I got a letter from your father tha was rote the 4 July and I got it the 5 of August. It was a long time a coming. I had bin to Richmond. Henry and John[16] is well as far as I no. I herd from them yesterday. Catharine I hav sent my liknes by Lewis G Maness and my money also. I put in the letter that I sent by Lewis 60 dollars but I sent 67 dollars to you and if you are afraid to keep it at home you can get some body to keep it for you. Catharine I think you had beter pay Isaac Williams[17] for your cow. You can get father to do that for you.

Catharine I am afraid that we shal hav another battle before long. Tha are fixing for it now and we shal fight if the Yankees comes out to us. I do hope tha will let us alone. I can here some cannon down the river every day. Tha had a little skirmish last Sonday. There was some two or three kild. Catharine the boys has not come yet and I dont no what to think. Samuel Stewart[18] went after them and he has never come back yet. The boys said in there letter of the 28 that he come and took there names and went to Raleigh and tha had not seen him sinc. I hav herd that there has went a great many through Petersburg going to Richmond and I am afraid tha will go there. I do wish tha cold come

Chapter Two

here for I do want to see them so bad.[19] Catharine when Lewis Maness shook hands with me I shed tears. I hated to see him leav. He eat dinner with me and I told (*him*) to tel you that was some of my cooking. I can make up wheet dough and bake rite good bread.

Catharine I hav one hundred and forty five dollars of money sinc I come in camp and I hav sent you one hundred and seven dollars and I hav 18 dollars now. It taks so much money to by paper and stamps and invelops and washing my cloths. Catharine there is no chanc for me to come home now but I hope there will be after a while if I am spard to liv. I do hop and pray that I shal get home to see my loving and blesed little children again. May the good Lord help me I pray.

Catharine I am so uneasy about you now. You hav so much to do. I am afraid you will hurt your self. Catharine do the best you can. I do hope you will hav friends when you need them. I do hop that Miss Cox[20] will come and stay with you when you need her. I do wish I cold come home then but I am afraid I cant. I do hop you can get some body to stay with you and help you when you cant help your self. May the good Lord help you I pray. Rite soon and fail not.

Catharine the Negros[21] comes in the camp with baskets with pies and apples and any thing that you want but tha ask more for them than I will giv. Tha want all of our money and all of our help. I dont like these Viginians much. I think tha are cowards.[22] Catharine I shal need some cloths after a while if I dont get to come home. It seems like I shant get any more here.

William Henry my dear little son you must be a good (*boy*) and help your mother and feed your little horse tel I come home. My dear little son I want to see you so bad. Nancy Elizabeth my dear little daughter be a good girl. Mary Jane my dear little daughter be a good girl. Joseph Gibs my blesed little bab Lord bles the children I pray. My dear loving wife and little (*children*) fairwell for this time. Pray for me.

       Matthew C Yow to Nancy C Yow

Matthew C Yow October the 5: 1862
October the 5 the Sabbath

Dear Wife and Little Children

 I one more time take my pin in hand to rite you a few lines to let you no that I am alive yet but not vary well. I hav had a bad spel of the yellow jangers[23]. We left the Rappadan River the first day of September for Manasses and when we got there the battle was over.[24] We then started for Maryland and I got in four miles of the Potomac River and I giv out and tha sent me back to the hospital and it has bin 4 weeks to day sinc I left them and I am on my way to them now. I am in the vally over Blue Ridge. I hav (*not*) had chanc to rite to you so long I no you think I am dead but thank the Lord I am alive yet and I do hop and pray when this comes to hand it may find you all well.

 Catharine I receivd your letter of the 23: the 7 of September and fatheres the same time. When I turnd back I met Capt Dowd and he giv them to me and I want to here from you so bad I dont no what to do. I think when I get to the regiment tha will be a letter there for me. I hop tha will. My regiment is at Winchester now and I am on my way there and I sat down to rest and I thought I wold rite for I am in so much trouble. It seems lik I cant stand it much longer. I dream so much about you and the dear little children. It seems lik it will brak my hart. It seems lik I never shal get home any more. Catharine my loving wife I do want to see you and my dear little (*children*) so bad. I

Chapter Two

dont no what I shal do if I cant get to see you all one time more. I am praying day and night for you.

Catharine I will rite again as soon as I can and I want you and father to rite to me as often as you can. Direct your letter to Winchester VA. But I cant tel how long tha will stay there. Tha may be gon when I get there. I am in so much trouble that I dont no what to rite to you now. I can tel you that I am brok down and I dont think I can do much more. The men is nearly all brok down and I am afraid the Yankees will whip us yet. I expect there will be a battle at Winchester before long. Catharine I do want to here from you so bad I cant rest day nor night. Catharine I hav not seen your brothers in a long time and I haint herd from my brothers sinc I got fathers letter. I want to here from them. Matthew C Yow to Nancy C Yow his dear wife

Catharine My dear wife I am praying that we may meet again in this world and I hop you are praying for me that I may liv to get home to see you all one time more in this world. May the Lord bles and sav us all forever. So fairwell my dear wife and little children.

Matthew C Yow to Nancy C Yow

October the 28: 1862
Matthew C Yow

Dear Wife and Little Children

I one time more take my pen in hand to rite you a few lines to let you no that I am well at this time and I do hop and pray that this may find you all well. I receivd your kind letter yesterday the 27. I was so glad to here from you again for I was so uneasy I cold not rest night nor day. I am going to send this letter by Capt Dowd. He is coming to see you and get some cloths for me. I want you to send me one good suit of cloths and my overcoat. I want 2 pare of galloos[25] for I am almost naked and nearly perrish. I dont get half enogt to eat and it goes hard with me for I always had plenty at home. You may no it is a bad chanc here.

Catharine I want you rite a letter and send back by Dowd and tel me all about the cloths. Catharine my dear wife I cant rite much this time. You said you wanted to name the baby Matthew. I am willing. I hav rote to you what to name him. If it wold suit you John Matthew. I do want to see him so bad and all the rest of the dear little children but seems lik I never shal get there any more. I pray to the Lord night and day that I may get home to see you all again and I hop you will pray for me. I am in a heep of trouble about you and the children. I am here in the mountians and the wether vary cold. Catharine tel my dear old father to rite me a ful letter and send by Dowd. I want to here all about the times there.

Catharine I want you to get lether and hav shoes made for you and the children. I want them to hav shoes. Henry must hav shoes. I want you to rite to me all about your things your hogs and cattle and how much corn you made. I want to no if you are out of bacon yet and how much meet you can mak this fall. You must do the best you can and be saving for the hard times has not come yet. I dont no what you will do for salt. You and father must try to get some if you can. Catharine I will rite again as soon as I can and tel you more than I can now.

William Henry my dear little son you must be a good boy and help your mother and reed your book. Lord bles the dear children.

Catharine I must close for this time by saying I stil remain your husband tel death. pray for me my dear wife. So fairwell for this time. Nancy C Yow rite as often as you can.

Chapter Two

∼

Fredericsburg VA November the 30: 1862
Matthew C Yow

Dear Wife and Little Children

    I this blesed Sabbath day tak my pen to rite you a few lines to let you no that I am well at this time and I do hop when this comes to hand it may find you all in good helth. Catharine Capt Dowd has come back and brought me a letter from you and father. I was so glad to here from you all one time more. He did not bring our cloths to us. He left them in Richmond and I dont no when we shal get them. We hav bin here 9 days expecting a battle and it has not come on yet and I hop it wont.[26]

    Catharine am in a heep of trouble sinc fathers barn was burnd.[27] I am afraid tha will do somthing to your things. I do hop tha will not pester you but I no they are not two good to burn your barn and wheet. I hav rot 2 or 3 letters to you and father sinc Dowd went home. I hop you hav got them. We hav hard times here and I think you hav bad times there. We are all in trouble. Some times I get so bad out of hart that I dont no what to do when I think of you and the pore little children. It seems like it will brak my hart for it seems like there is no chanc for me to come home soon. Tha wont giv no furlows to well men and if tha dont tha will all runaway. The men sa tha will go home to see there people and I can tel you the men will not fight as tha hav fought the way tha (are) treted. We dont (get) enough to eat and the flour we get is sour and it is not fit to eat but we hav to eat it or none. Catharine I hate to tel you as bad as it is. I no it hurts your feelings.

    Catharine do the best you can and put your trust in the good Lord for all our help must come from him. Pray for me which I beleiv you do and I hop your prares will be herd and answerd.

Catharine my dear wife I do hop and pray that we may meet again in this world. If we never see each other on earth I do hop we will meet in haven. Catharine I shed tears and pray for you all. I never close my eys at night without asking the good Lord to bles and tak cear of me and I do thank the Lord that my helth has bin as good as what it has. Catharine I am in trouble but I trust in the Lord for my help. Catharine I do want to get the things that you sent to me and the potatoes and unions that the dear little children sent to me. Bles there dear soles. I do want to see them so bad. I do hop that we will get back to NC but I am afraid we shal hav to (*stay*) out here all winter without any tents and it will kil us all. there is lots of men here barefoot and the wether is vary cold.[28] I can tel you a soldiers life is a hard one you may be sure.

Catharine I was sorrow when you said you had no wheet sowd yet. I am a fraid you wont get none sowd. I dont no what you will if you dont. Father said in his letter that you did not hav half corn enough to do you. He said he wold hav to go to Stanly to buy corn for you or let the children suffer.[29] Catharine you hav got money and you must giv it to him to buy corn. I no he will do the best he can for you. Catharine tel my old granfather that I hav not forgoten him yet. I do want to see him. Tel him to pray for me. May the lord bles and sav you all is my prare so no more.

Catharine giv my best respect to all my friends. Tel them I want to see them all. Tel all of my brothers and sisters that I hav not forgoten them. I want to see them. If I cold I wold rite them all a letter. O that I cold see you all and talk with you one more time in this world. I shal never die satisfied without I do see you all again. I cant rite as I cold talk to you.

Catharine when this you see remember me though many miles apart we be. Catharine tel your father I dont get any letters from him. I hav rote several and got no answer from them.

Chapter Two

Catharine I must bring my letter to a close for this time by saying I stil remain your affectionate husband until death shal part us.

    Matthew C Yow To Nancy C Yow

    William H Yow

    Nancy E Yow

    Mary J Yow

    Joseph G Yow

    John M Yow

My dear wife and dear little children fairwell for this time.

    Nancy C Yow

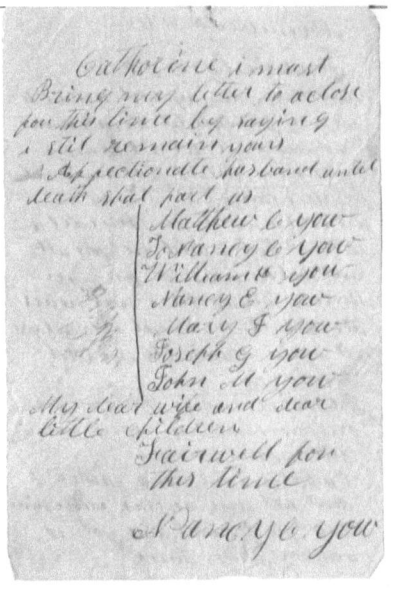

This last part of Matthew's letter dated November 30, 1862, shows his whimsical way of writing the names of his wife and children at the close of some of his letters (image courtesy of Larry R. Yow).

Matthew C you to
Nancy C you
Catharine I will let you where we are
now we all in camp on the railroad at
a place cald Burgaw 23 miles from
Wilmington and I hear that we was
under marching orders but I can't tell
how true it is   Catharine you said that
you war in so much trouble I no you
are I want you to do the best you can
and put your trust in the good Lord
and he will help you in time of trouble
Catharine I am praying for you and the
Dear little children and I hop and
Beliew that he will here and answer my
prair I can tell you I am in trouble
But I trust in the good Lord for help and
tell that trust in him he will bless
I am amongst all sorts of people and I
have hard trials but let others do as
tha may I will serv my god I have one
testament and two him Books and I read
them every chanc I get you said you
wisht I cold see little John I do wish I
cold see him and all the rest Also you

This is the second page of a letter to Catharine and the children dated February 15, 1863. In this letter Matthew encouraged Catharine to trust in the Lord during their "time of trouble"
(Image courtesy of Larry R. Yow).

Chapter Three
January 18 – April 21, 1863

"I stil hav a hope that I may get bak to you and the dear little children again."

Times were perilous and there was much despair for Matthew at camp and for Catharine and the children on the home front. During this time, there was also hope. Matthew chose hope over despair and often wrote to Catharine about the things he hoped for: that his friends would help save the wheat and oats, that his family would write more, and that the Yankees would "leave us alone." Most importantly Matthew hoped for the things that pertained to his wife and little children. In almost every letter to them, he wrote of his deep desire to be reunited with them. He never gave up hope that he would see Catharine again in this life, but if not, then he would see her in heaven where they would part no more.

From Matthew's first letter to the last one, hope appears to be a virtue that he relied on every hour and every day. There were times when Matthew's situation was so bleak that hope was all there was and he clung to it tenaciously. Matthew was surely an example to those around him as he lived his Christian faith in those adverse circumstances. He wrote to Catharine in February 1863, "I am amongst all sorts of people and I hav hard trials but let others do as tha may I will serv my God." Matthew filled his letters with the ways he cultivated his faith; he wrote about how he read from his two hymn books and his New Testament every chance he got. In his letters, he informed Catharine about the chaplains in his brigade and the revival meetings in the Confederate camps. He expressed hope that she had such meetings at home to help sustain her faith.

Matthew was always hopeful but there were moments of doubt when he wondered if prayer would carry him through. Sometimes his faith wavered. Matthew must have been exasperated as he wrote home several times about praying for peace with such remarks as "... it seems to do no good." Another time he shared that the more he prayed, the more people fought! Matthew, as well as all the people of his generation, North and South, had to grapple with the mysteries of God and such questions as why He would allow such devastation on His people. Perhaps Matthew pondered the "causes, course, and consequences" of the war or perhaps he did not. Maybe he was one of many of his generation who, "...simply looked to their religious faith for consolation, if not understanding."[1]

Matthew had posed for a picture while he was in Petersburg during the summer of 1862. Unlike many Civil War photographs with soldiers brandishing their weapons, the image of Matthew presents a stark contrast. He was photographed sitting near a table with one hand resting on what appears to be his New Testament or another book and a Bible in the pocket of his jacket. He chose an image consistent with who he was so his family would remember him the way he was – as a loving husband and father striving to be faithful to God while hoping and praying always for his family's very best.

Chapter Three

In the following letters, we see a still hopeful but frustrated soldier longing for a furlough after almost a year of service. In the last letter in this chapter, Matthew wrote that he had good reason to hope for a soon reunion with his wife and children. Not long after that letter he was on his way home to see his family "... one more time in this world."

∼

Goldsboro NC
January 18: 1863

Dear Wife and Little Children

I tak my pen in hand to let you no where I am. I am at Goldsboro NC one time more and I am well and I do hop when this comes to hand it may find you well. We landed here yesterday but cant tel how long we shal stay. I think we shal go to Wilmington. Tha say the Yankees is going to try that place and if tha do there will be some hard fiting done for we hav a great many men here now.[2]

Catharine I got a letter from you the 2 of January ---- that I hav had sinc Dowd come back and ---- letters and I am afraid you never get them. The chanc has bin bad to get letters from you for we hav bin marching so much. I do hop you will get this and I think we will get letters now. Matthew C Yow

I got a letter from your father the same day that I got yours. I hav not got no letter from my father sinc Dowd come back. I want him to rite and let me no how he is geting along these hard times. Catharine I herd this morning that there was 5 regiments of Yankees at New Burn[3] laid down there arms and said tha wold not fight no more against us. I cant tel how true it is.

Catharine I cant tel you when I can come home. It seems like I never shal get to see you and my dear little children any more. I want you to do the best you can and pray for pore me that I may get home to see you all one more time in this world. I have praid for the good Lord to protect and save me and I do hop he will hear and answer my prares. May the good Lord bles and save us all forever. Catharine rite when you get this so fairwell my dear wife Nancy C Yow

~

New Hanover County NC
February the 1: 1863   M C Yow

My Dear Wife and Little Children

    I one more time take my pen to rite you a few lines to let you no that I am well at this time and I do hop when this comes to hand it may find you all well. Catharine I rote you a letter the 18 of January when I was at Goldsboro and I hav bin looking for a letter from you for some time and I hav not got no answer yet. I hav not had no letter from you sinc the 2 of January and I do want to here from you so bad I dont no what to do. Catharine I cant tel what is the matter. We left Goldsboro the 17: and marcht to a place called South Washington ---- miles from Willmington and this morning we marcht 6 or 7 miles nearer to Willmington on the railrode and I cant tel how long we shal stay here but not long I no. I expect we shal get into a fight before long but I cant tel what we are going to do.

    We are always marching through rain and mud and water. We see hard times you may be sure but sinc we come to NC we hav enough to eat such as bread and meat and we hav some potatoes. We hav bin drawing fresh pork and it eats mity good to me. Catharine I am fat. Uncle John Stuts[4] says I am fatter than he ever seed me. I am as harty as I ever was in my life and I am so thankful that I am for it is so bad to be sick in camp. Catharine I

Chapter Three

cant tel you where you had beter direct your letters but I think you had beter send them to Goldsboro and tha will come to me. Direct to Goldsboro NC General Cooks[5] Brigade Co D the 48 regiment NC Troops in cear of Capt Dowd. Catharine if you get this letter I want you to rite to me and I want father to rite to me and John Manes[6] and W N Brower. I want to here from them all.

M C Yow

Matthew C Yow to his dear Wife Nancy C Yow and little children Catharine I think there be some chanc to get to come home this spring. Colonel Hill says if them that has runaway will come back by the 10 of this month tha will not be punisht and if tha dont tha will be shot without any trial. And tha had beter come. If tha will come back we will get furlows. James Morgan[7] is at home now. Colonel Hill has come back again and he says we all shal go home to see our families. I do hop and pray that I can come to see you and the children one more time in this world. May the good Lord bles and sav us all for ever. Catharine dont forget to pray and pray for me that I may be spard to get back again.

Catharine I want rite to me whether brother Jones is gon back or not. I want to rite to them and I dont no where to rite. But I suppose tha hav gon bak to Raleigh. I do want to see them so bad. Your brothers has come to NC but I dont no where tha are. We dont stay in one plac long enough to here from any of you. Catharine I want you to right as often as you can. I want to here from you. If I cold get to any place that I cold stay any time I cold rite to you where to send your letters. I must close for this time.

Catharine My dear wife do the best you can. I am praying

for you and my dear little children that you may not suffer. May the good Lord bles and sav us all for ever is my prare.

    Matthew C Yow to Nancy C Yow fairwell

New Hanover County February 15 1863
Nancy C Yow M C Yow

Dear Wife and Little Children

 I one more time tak my pen in hand to drop you a few lines to let you no that I am well at this time and I do hop when this comes to hand it may find you all in good helth. Catharine I receivd your vary kind letter last night wich was great satisfaction to me to here from you one time more. I was so uneasy that I cold not rest at all. I hav not had no letter from you sinc the 2 day of January and you may no that I was uneasy. I rote you a letter the 1 of this month and on the 8 and I hop you will get them all.[8] Catharine you said that you wanted me to come home. I think I will get a furlo to come before long. I do not want to runaway if tha will giv me half a chanc. James Morgan and Georg Camel[9] is at home on furlo and some is going every day. Colonel Hill says we shal all go to see our families but I am a fraid we shant all get to go. Matthew C Yow Nancy C Yow

 Catharine I will tel you where we are now. We are in camp on the railrode at a place cald Burgaw 22 miles from Wilmington and I herd that we was under marching orders but I cant tel how true it is. Catharine you said that you was in so much trouble. I no you are. I want you to do the best you can and put your trust in the good Lord and he will help you in time of trouble.

 Catharine I am praying for you and the dear little children and I hop and believ that he will here and answer my prare. I

Chapter Three

can tel you I am in trouble but I trust in the good Lord for help and all that trust in Him He will bless. I am amongst all sorts of people and I hav hard trials but let others do as tha may I will serv my God. I hav one Testament and two him books and I read them every chanc I get. You said you wisht I cold see little John.[10] I do wish I cold see him and all the rest.

M C Yow

∼

Febuary the 27 1863
Pocotaligo South Carolina   Matthew C. Yow

Dear Wife and Little Children

 I one more time tak my pen in hand to drop you a few lines to let you no that I am well at this time and I do hop when this comes to hand it may find you and the dear little children well. Catharine I receivd your vary kind letter yesterday the 26 that you rote the 15. Catharine I was so glad to here that you was all well. I shal look for more letters soon. I hav Rote 4 or 5 in this month and I hop tha all will get to you. I Rote one sinc I come to this place the 24.[11] I hop you will get it. Catharine you said in your letter that Monrow Garner[12] wanted to By Henrys colt Colonel Walker. I dont want you to sel him yet. I do hop and pray that I will get home again. Henry wants to keep him and I want him to keep his colt.

 Catharine you said that you wanted me to come home and help you plant your Irish potatoes. I am a fraid I cant get home that soon. We hav got so far off down here in the swamps. Our regiment is vary helthy at this time but I am a fraid it wont be so long in these moosy swamps. Catharine you said that you made a good crop of Irish potatoes last year. You said that you thought you had 11 bushels now. Take cear of them. Tha will bring you 4 or 5 dollars per bushel this spring. Catharine we dont fare as well in South Carolina as we did in NC. We get beef here and not much of that. We hav got some pork. I think if we hav to stay here long we shal see hard times. But that is what we are use to is hard times. I cant tel whether we shal hav any fight here or not. Some thinks we will and if we do it will be in a few days. I do hop the fiting is nearly over. I dont think it can last much longer.

Catharine Jones said in his letter that he was going back to his company and I was glad to here that for I want him to go to his company. He said that Isaac was not going back if he cold help it. I think he had beter go. If he dont tha will tak him up and punish him and tha may kill him. I want them both to go back and do there duty as soldiers. I started home one time but I was perswaded to do that and if I had got home I did not aim to try to stay there.[13] I was sick and I wanted to see you and the dear little children and try to get some body to sow some wheet for you. But I did not get to see you at that time. But I do hop that the good Lord will spare my life that I may get home to see you all one time more. That has bin my prare all the time and I do hop that the Lord has herd my prares. Catharine I belev you are praying for me.

Catharine I will say to you that my Uncle John H Stuts and his son Henry W Stuts[14] is here with me and tha are both well at this time. Henry W Stuts has had the smallpox vary bad. Catharine said in your letter that you was so lonsom. I no you are. I am so sorrow for you that I cant hardly stand it. Catharine my dear and loving wife put your trust in the Lord who can sav you. Tel father to rite to me as soon as he can. Tel Elisabeth R Yow[15] that I hav not forgoten her yet. It has bin 11 months sinc I saw her. So I must close for this time. Dear father and Mother fairwell for this time. Catharine my dear wife and dear little (*children*) fairwell for this time.

Matthew C Yow

Chapter Three

Nancy C Yow
William Henry Be a good (*boy*) and obey your Mother.

Catharine,[16]

Cousin Henry W Stuts is here with me and he has had the smallpox[17] and if you get I will tel you what he said tha don for him. He said that you must not eat no greas from the time it begins to brak out tel the scabs get dry. Eat wheet bread and coffee and be sure to keep warm. Dont let the are get to you at all. Uncle John H Stuts is here and him and Henry is both well at this time. Give my love to all my friends. Tel father to rite.

 Catharine My dear wife I do want to see you and the dear little (*children*) so bad but it seems like I never shal get home any more. But I shal hop and pray to the good Lord that I may come to you again in this world. William Henry my dear little son obey your mother and be a good boy. Read your book. Nancy E Yow Mary J Yow Joseph G Yow John M Yow so my dear little children fairwell.
      Matthew C Yow Nancy C Yow

Pocotaligo SC March the 8 1863
Matthew C Yow to Joseph Albright

Dear Father and Mother[18]
 It is with plesure that I seat myself to drop you a few lines to inform you that I am well at present truly hoping when this comes to hand it may find you all in good helth. I receivd your vary kind letter the 6 inst[19] Which giv me great satisfaction to

here from you all one time more. I hav receivd several letters from Catharine sinc I hav bin here. She rits to me that she sees hard times and I am so sorrow for her. I no that she is in much trouble for she never was use to having every to see two and I am afraid that she will try to do more than she is able to do. I study a greateal about them. I do not no what tha will do if I cant soon get home before long. You said in your letter that the conscripts and deserters is stil doing mischief yet I wish tha wold all come to the army and not hav so much fus in the contry. It seems lik the people is trying to see what tha can do. I am looking for a letter from Catharine to day. Matthew C Yow

We herd here yesterday that the Yankees was firing on Fort Sumter all day and I hav herd some heavy cannoning to day but I hav not herd what was don. I hop that if tha come out here we will whip them and I hop that will end the war. The war commenct at Charlston and I hop it will end ther. I hav no news of any importanc to rite to you at this time. I am afraid that this to swampy contry will not agree with me if we stay here much longer. The wether is vary changeable for some times it is vary and in a short time it will be cold enough to freeze. But the woods here is green now. Last Sunday morning there was a big frost here and it is vary cool to day. I want to rite to Henry and John but I dont no wher to rite. We hav hard time here. We hav to drill twise every day one company drill and one battalion drill and parade in the evening and not much to eat here. The men greiv vary bad at the fare. So I must close for this time by saying pray for me when it goes well with you. Yours truly so fairwell for this time.

M C Yow to Mr Joseph Albright

Chapter Three

Pocotaligo SC March the 19 1863
Mrs Nancy C Yow

My Dear Wife and Little Children

It is with plesure I seat myself to try to rite you a few lines to let you no that I am well at this time truly hoping when this comes to hand it may find you all well. Catharine I receivd your vary kind letter the 17 that you (*wrote*) the 9 and 22 Febu. I was so glad to here from you again. Catharine I rote you a letter the 17 and sent it off and got yours the same day.[20] You said that I did not tel you where to direct your letters. Direct to Pocotaligo SC. I cant tel how long we shal stay here. We are throwing up breastworks here every day and tha say it will take us 10 days. Yet I do not think that we shal hav a fight here tho we may. Catharine you said that Mrs Williamson wanted to no if I knew any thing of her son John. he was taken sick and sent to the hospital at Petersburg and I haint herd sinc.

My dear wife I cant tel you when I can come home. Tha wil not giv furloes now. It seems like tha dont intend to let us go home any more. I dont think tha use us right. We hav bin out here almost 12 months and cant get to go to see our wives and dear little children. I think that's rong. I now tha cold let us come if tha wold but the big men dont cear for us. Tha go home when tha pleas. Catharine you said that the boys was gon back. I am glad tha went. I now tha cold not stay there in peac. I do hop that peac will be made before long so we pore suffering soldiers can return to there homes and lovd ones. Catharine you said that you seed so much trouble. I no you do. I want you to try to bear it as well as you can. I see trouble two but I trust in the good Lord for help. I do thank my god for giving me good helth. It seems like I hav bin blest. I do hop by the aid of your prares I shal return to you again my dear wife Nancy C Yow.

I Hope You Will All Remember Me

~

Pocotaligo SC April the 5 1863
Matthew C Yow to Nancy C Yow

My Dear Wife and Little Children

 Through the mercies of our hevenly Father I this blesed Sabbath evning I seat myself to drop you a few lines to inform you that I am well at present truly hoping when this comes to hand it may find you all in good helth. Catharine I receid your vary kind letter under date of the 24 March. I was truly glad to here from you and the dear little children. You said in that letter that you didnot get a letter that week but father got one and sent it to you to read and then you rote that letter.

 I receivd your letter when I was riting to father and I made mension of it in his letter of the 1 April. Catharine I expect we shal leav here in a short time. We hav marching orders now to be ready at any time to go to Charlston. It is thought that the Yankees is going to make an atact on Charlston but I cant tel how it will be yet.[21]

 Catharine you said in your letter that you see hard times. I no you do. I am sorrow for you and I want to be there to do my things again but it seems like I never shal get home any more but I stil hav a hop that I may get bak to you and the dear little children again. That is my prare and has bin all the time and I believ that you are praying for me all the time.

 Catharine today is Easter I suppose. O that I cold be with you and my dear little children. Pore little children I expect tha hav forgotten me almost. I hav bin gone so long. Catharine father says the children looks so well. Lord bles them I pray. I cant rite much this time. I will rite as often as I can. I rote your father a letter sinc I come here and I rote one to your brother William[22] and one to John Maness. I rote you a letter the 24 and I put a

Chapter Three

ring in it and 50 cents in money.[23] I want to no if you get them. If you get them I will send Nancy and Jane one. So I must close by saying to you to remember me in your prares. I stil remain your affectionate husband until death parts us. So Fairwell Nancy C Yow.

~

Pocotaligo SC
April the 21 1863 M C Yow

My Dear Wife and Little Children

It is with much pleasure that I tak my pen to drop you a few lines to inform you that I am well at present truly hoping when this comes to hand it may find you all well. Catharine I receivd a letter from you last week the one you rote the 6 of April and I did not rite bak to you tel now. I sent a letter by David D Yow[24] and he did not get off as soon as I expected and I thought I wold rite this morning and see which wold get home first David or the letter. He is going to leav this morning. Catharine I hav sent my overcoat by him and 50 cents worth of pins and one dollars worth of needles and one dollars worth of stamps and one camp him book and a cap for little Joseph Gibbs. And I sent father and William Henry 20 buttons to put on there coats and David Yow did not hav money to tak him back and I let him 3 dollars and if he dont spend it he will giv it to you. I told him to pay himself for his troubles with my things. I hav nothing to send to Nancy and Jane but some pins and needles.

Catharine I will say to you that my brother Isaac come to see me last Sunday the 19. I was so glad to see him. Jones did not get to come. He was detaild to go to Charlston on some bisnis. I want to go to see him before long. The boys seems to be vary well satisfied now more so than tha was at Camp Homes.[25]

Catharine I must tell you what I way 155 pounds yesterday. that is 20 pounds more than when I left home. I am in good helth at this time and I am so thankful for it. All is quiet here now and I do hop that peac will be made soon so we pore soldiers can come home to those that is near and dear to us. O that I cold come to see you all again. I do want to come to see you and help you plant corn. I do hop tha will giv furlows again before long. I no tha cold if tha wold. I want you to rite me all the news and rite as often as you can. I am looking for a letter from you now.

Catharine sinc I commenct this letter I hav herd that there going 4 men out of every company home on furlows. If that be so I think I will get to come before long. So I must close for this time by saying I stil remain your affectionate (*husband*) until death.

So fairwell dear wife Nancy C Yow

Chapter Four
June 17 - August 30, 1863

"The men is all out of hart and tha are runing away in a huree"

North Carolina has the reputation of having had more deserters during the war than any other state. It was estimated soon after the war that 23,000 North Carolina soldiers had deserted between 1861 and 1865. This number has been challenged by historians and the generally accepted number is now about 14,000 troops[1] which would mean that the soldiers of the Tar Heel state did not desert at a greater rate than the soldiers of other states, North or South. Although we do not know the exact number of desertions due to incomplete records and a myriad of other reasons, we do know that the issue was cause for concern. In mid-1862, the Confederate war secretary, George W. Randolph, correlated the weakness of the armies to the number of men deserting.[2] Lt. Colonel Walkup wrote a letter to Governor Vance in October of 1862 about how the lack of clothing, shoes, blankets, and food was related to the number of men absent from camp.[3]

I Hope You Will All Remember Me

Diaries and letters written to loved ones at home documented some of the reasons that soldiers left camp without leave. A lack of necessities, worrying about family, few furloughs, and believing that it was a rich man's war but a poor man's fight, were some of the reasons men chose to leave the ranks. Leaving did not always indicate a lack of loyalty to the cause; sometimes it was just a matter of what was best for the soldier's family.[4]

Matthew's letters echo these sentiments. In the fall of 1862, Matthew wrote about the sour food, shoeless comrades, and lack of basic needs. In a November letter, he wrote about men running away because they were unable to get furloughs. Matthew was disappointed that "the big men" could visit their families anytime but he and the other privates could not. He expressed his war weariness by writing he was "out of hart." After the Confederate losses at Gettysburg and Vicksburg in the summer of 1863, feelings of hopelessness pervaded the armies, and desertions increased.

Catharine's letters to Matthew, although we can only speculate about the contents based on his letters to her, were much like the ones many wives wrote to their husbands. They told of the hardships at home such as food shortages and lawlessness. Matthew received letters from Catharine asking him to come home to plant potatoes and defend his home. He was ambivalent as to which choice to make – to stay or go. In an August 1863 letter to Catharine, he wrote, "Sometimes I hav a great mind to come home for I no that it will be no credit to me to sta and get kild." From the letters we can infer that Matthew's decision making was influenced by the grim reality of the consequences should he be captured and found guilty of desertion. In a January 1864 letter to Catharine, Matthew wrote about being forced, along with his entire brigade, to watch the execution of a fellow comrade by firing squad; his crime was desertion. Perhaps

Chapter Four

Matthew wondered which choice, staying or leaving, would give him the greater chance to get back home to his family.

Governor Vance wrote to a friend in September of 1864 about his disappointment concerning the way the war was going. Perhaps he was thinking of desertion when he wrote, "The great popular heart is not now and never has been in this war. It was a revolution of the politicians, not the people."[5]

June the 17 1863 M C Yow
Mrs Nancy C Yow

My Dear Wife and Little Children

Through the kind hand of Providenc I hav bin spard to seat myself to drop you a few lines to let you no that I am well at present truly hoping when this comes to hand it may find you and the dear little children well and harty. Catharine I hav not herd from you sinc I left you at High Point[6] and I want to here vary bad. I am looking for a letter from you now. I hop I will get one soon. I wrote to you the day I got to the company and I wrote to father sinc and I thought I wold write to you again to day and let you no where I am now. We are in camp about 4 miles east of Richmond near the 7 pines where we fought the Yankees last June.[7] But I dont here any tel of a fight here now. I dont no what we come here for but I suppose to wach for them.

Catharine I here some nuse in camp to day that we shal hav to go to Vicksburg in Missisippi and I can tel you that I dont want to go there you may be sure. We hav bin sent here to gard this point. It was thought that the Yankees wold mak another rade run here. Tha come out down here and stold some horces and cattle and sheep and burnt some houses and then tha went back and tha may come out again. I cant tel. Our boys has bin down on the old battlefield and brought some old Yankee bones to camp.[8] Tha say that the Yankees is lying down there any where dryd. I no that looks bad. I hav not bin to the battlefield yet. I am going down if we stay here. I think I will tomorrow and see the place where pore Andrew Stuts got his leg shot off. Catharine I study so much about you and the dear little (*children*). It seems like I cant stand it now.

June the 18 63

    Catharine, I will say to you that I hav bin on the battle field today and I saw 7 skul bones in one pile besids may others ling about. Any wheres it is an awful looking sight you may be sure.[9] Catharine Henry W Stuts is going to start home to day and he may go to see you. I cant tel. He talks like going by High Point and if he does he will go by fathers I expect.
    Catharine I will say to you that my 2 brothers will be in our company before tomorrow night.[10] There is 2 men in our company that is going to the 15. I think it will be a swap this time if nothing happens more than I no. Catharine I hav sent for a pocket Bible. I hav red my testament all the time and I thought I wold get a Bible and read that. It is some satisfaction to read the blesed promises in this Bible. My book and hart shal never part. M C Yow
    Catharine I suppose there has bin a big (*fight*) in western Va over in the vally at Winchester.[11] I no the place vary well. We whipt them bad. We taken 8 thousand prisnors and 70 pecies of artillery and every thing that tha had. We hav a heep of camp nuse here. Some think we will go to Vicksburg and some say we will go to South Carolina again but I dont no where we will go. Catharine I hav nothing more to rite at this time. I stil remain your true and loving husband untel death.

Chapter Four

Matthew C Yow to Mrs Nancy C Yow. I hav nothing at this time. I am looking for a letter from you. I want to here so bad.

So fairwell my dear wife Nancy C Yow. M C Yow
William H. Yow
Nancy E. Yow
Mary J. Yow
Joseph G. Yow
John M. Yow

My dear little children so fairwell. Lord bles the children.

Camp near Richmond VA
July the 3 63 M. C. Yow

My Dear Wife and Little Children

I one time more seat my self to drop you a few lines to let you no that I am well at present truly hoping when comes to hand it may find you all well and harty. Catharine I receivd your vary welcom letter yesterday the 2 inst under date of June the 23 and you said in your letter that that you had riten 3 letters to me sinc I left you and I hav not got but 2 of them. Your 2 letter has not come to me yet and I was geting so uneasy I cold not rest. Wensday the 1 our company was sent off on picket down on Chickahomine River and I was there when I got the letter which give me great releif. But I was vary sorrow to here that your wheet was ripe and you cold not get it cut. If you cant get it saved I dont no what you will do. I am afraid you and the dear little children will suffer and I cant stand that you no. Mrs Nancy C. Yow

Catharine the same day that we went off on picket the regiment was orderd off two. And we expect to hav a big battle here again but the Yankees wold not fight much. General Cooks brigade did not get in the skirmish. Tha had some vary heavy cannonding but not much harm don. Tha Yankees ran and we hav just got bak to camp. But tha may try us again. I cant tel.[12] I hav not seen my 2 brothers in 3 days. I saw the regiment to day but there company was on picket. I dont no whether tha hav come yet or not. I am going to see if tha have come this eavning. I hav bin looking for a letter from father but he has had so much to do that he cold not write. I want to here how tha are geting on taking the out liers. Tel my old granfather that I hav not forgoten him yet. I want him to pray for me when it goes well with him. Our company is in vary good helth at this time. I do hop it will remain so while we are here in old Va.

Catharine I am so glad that you hav got some beter. You said that had a bad risen under your arm. I no how bad that is but it will get well I hop soon. Catharine you are vary week and I dont want you to try to do so much and lay your self up. You say that you are in so much trouble and I bliev you are. I no I am my self. But I dont want you to greav so much about me. I am afraid you will injure your self. I no it is hard enough to brak our harts to be seperated like we are now. But I do hop and pray that the good Lord will spare my life and yours two that we may meet again in this world.

Catharine you and the children is on my mind so much that I dream of seeing you every night. I saw you all last night as plain as I ever did. when I dream so much it makes me uneasy about you and my dear little children. Catharine I want to no if you hav had much rain. It has bin raining here for the last 2 weeks and crops looks well here. M. C. Yow

Catharine I hav nothing more to rite at present. I will close my letter by saying to you rite soon. Also dont forget to pray. I stil remain your affectionate husband until death parts us. So fairwell for this time Nancy C Yow.

Chapter Four

A few lines to Elisabeth R. Yow[13]

Dear Mother

    I seat my self to drop you a few lines to let you no that I am well at present truly hoping when this comes to hand it may find you and family well. Betsy I will say to you that I saw your brother Henry Maness[14] the 1 day of July. I staid with him nearly all day. He told me to rite to you and say to you that he was well now but he had bin sick. He said his family was well the last he herd from them. He said that he wold rite to you before long. He belongs to the cavalry from SC Halcamess legion Co A. So I must close for this time. Rite soon so fairwell for this time Elisabeth R. Yow.

M. C. Yow

Mrs Nancy C Yow
July the 18 1863

My Dear Wife and Little Children

    Through the kind merces of our heavenly Father I hav bin one time more permited to drop you a few lines to inform you that I am well at present and I do hop and pray when this comes to hand it may find you and the dear little children all well and harty. Catharine I receivd your vary welcom letter the 16 that you wrote the 7. I was so glad to here that you was well and harty one more time. I am some beter satisfied now than I hav bin. When I can here that you are all well it chers me up. I do hop you will be well now and can attend to your things.

I Hope You Will All Remember Me

Catharine I was writing to my dear old father when I got your letter and I did not write to you that day. I am looking for a letter from father now. I hav not had but one from him sinc I left. He said in that letter that he had rote one to me before that and I never got it. I hav got all of your letters I think.

Catharine you said that you expected that old Hy[15] had kild my boar. I do hate to here that but I no he is mean enough to do any thing. I do hop and pray to the good Lord that I may be spard to get home again. Any man that will do that may will do any thing. I think tha will steal as tha hav done. And there is big Dav. That great lawyer is going to law me as long as I liv. If he had wanted to law me so bad he ought come to see me when I was at home and I wold giv him something to law for. But I will stop this for such a tory[16] as Dav Williamson is not worth talking about.[17]

Catharine I am vary glad that you hav got some corn plowd at last. I am afraid it was hurt but it has raind so much that you cold not work. You say you hav got your potatos all planted. I was glad to here that. Catharine do the best you can and dont work two hard for I no you are not able to work much. You said that you had drawd 24 dollars sinc I left.[18] I no Lewis Maness will attend to you right. I believ he is a friend to me and he is to you. I will say to you that I hav drawd 25 dollars sinc I came back. Catharine I want you to rite to me how all your things is geting on. I hav (been) vary uneasy about your wheet. It raind so much and I was afraid it was not hauld in when the weet got in.

M C Yow

~

July the 30 1863
Mrs Nancy C Yow

Chapter Four

My Dear Wife

I am one more time permited to drop you a few lines informing you that I am not well but I feel some better than I did when I wrote last. I hav not bin well for several days and I hav fel at away tel I am as pore as you was when I was at home. I do hop when this comes to hand it may find you and the dear children well and harty. I was so glad to here that you had got wel and harty again. I do hop you will be well now. Catharine I wil say to you that I did not get no letter to day. I got one last Sunday but I answerd it and I thought I wold write to day. I am afraid I dont get all your letters. Catharine I haint much to write to you now. we are stil at the same camp yet and all is quiet now but I cant tel what a day may bring forth. I hav herd that tha are fiting in NC about Weldon.[19] We may hav to go their yet. M. C. Yow

Catharine I am here not wel and you may no that I am not satisfied here in this troublesom place. when I study so much about you and our dear little children it seems like I cant sta here much longer. You may be sure that I dont see any satisfaction here. The men is all out of hart and tha are runing away in a huree now and I dont care if tha all go and that wold brak this unholy war. Catharine I am afraid that it is going to be sickly here. It rains so much. It rains here every day. I cant rite much at this time. I am looking for a letter now. I think I will get one soon. Catharine my dear wife do the best you can for your self and our dear little ones. Catharine dont forget to pray. May the good Lord bles and save us all forever. I stil remain your affectionate husband untel death.

Mrs Nancy C. Yow fairwell. Rite soon and fail not.

Catharine [20]

I cant here nothing from your brothers sinc that great battle in Penn.[21] I am afraid tha are kild or wounded. My 2 brothers is both well but tha are not satisfied. Tha are so tiard of the war. The soldiers is all tiard of it. Tha are running away from here. Like any thing the pore soldiers is out of hart the worst now that I hav out of hart now that I ever saw them. Yet tha all think we will have to giv it up and I think so myself. It looks so at any rate. I am out of hart myself at this time. Matthew C. Yow

Catharine I had 2 little rings made and I put them in a letter to Nancy Elisabeth and Mary Jane. I do hop tha will get them. C. A. Stutts[22] made them. Tha will pleas the dear little children. I also sent you 2 sheets of good paper in an envelop this week. I hop you will get it. It is good paper. I sent William Henry a peac of poetary in a letter this week. I want him to read that and be a good boy. I wish I cold send little Joseph Gibs and little John Matthew something but I haint nothing to send to them now. Lord sav my dear little children I pray.

M. C. Yow

Fredericksburg VA
August the 15 1863

Mrs Nancy C Yow my Dear Wife

It with plesure that I seat myself to drop you a few lines to let you no that I am wel at present truly hoping when this comes to hand it may find you and the dear children well and in beter hart than I am at this time. Catharine I receivd your welcom letter the 14 that you wrote the 8. I am glad to here that you are as wel as what you are. Pore little Nancy I am so sorrow for her. It seems like she has a hard time. I hop she wil soon get beter.

Chapter Four

Catharine you said that you was scard to liv by your self now. If you can get any body to liv with you that will do you any good I hav no objection. But I do hop that no one will pester you. You said that some one brok open Mr Wiat Williamson house.[23] It seems like tha wont let him alone. He ought to kil some of them.

I dont no what will become of our contry. The people has got to be so mean. It is the same way here. Some of them dont ceare what tha do. Their is two much meanness going on that we cant do any good. Thire is traitors every where and we shal be subjugated in spite of all we can do. I hav giv it up for lost. Sometimes I hav a great mind to come home for I no that it will be no credit to me to sta here and get kild and then be subgated by the Yankee rouges. I will say to you that I am out of hart. I wrote a letter to your father and I told him what I thought about this war and I dont think I am mistaken and I think that he will agree with me now. Our soldiers is all out of hart and there is a big battle depending some where about here. The Yankees is on one side of the river and we on the other. Tha come in sight some times and look over on our side. Tha kild one of our men the other day.

Catharine I was glad to here that your brothers was aliv and well. I was afraid tha was kild in that dredful battle.[24] My 2 brothers is both well. Tha got a letter from father yesterday. I cant tel what is the matter that I cant get no letter from father. I hav wrote several letters to him and no answer from him. I cant help but think that he has rote to me and I hav not got them. Catharine you said that Henry was at his granpapies a helping them thrash wheet. Pore little Henry I am glad that he can do something to help. I hop you can get your wheet cut now. I want (*you*) to tel me in your next letter how much old wheet you hav got yet. I do hop you wil hav plenty yet a while. Catharine tel my old granfather that I hav not forgoten him yet and I want to see him vary bad now but I cant tel when I shal see him again. I do hop it wont be long. I do hop and pray that my life will be spard so that I can return home you that is so near and dear to me. O that I cold see you all again and stay with you.

Catharine Read the 3 chapter of Isaiah and it will tel you about _____ Spirts. Also Read the 11 chapter of Daniel and see if it dont suit these times of trouble.[25]

Catharine I want you to do the best you can and you had beter sel your colt this fal if you can get the worth of him. He ought to bring you one hundred dollars. Father said that had bin offerd one hundred dollars for his colt and I no you ought to get that for your colt. Get all you can for him and I want to no what you are going to do with your cow if you hav turned her dry. Yet if tha dont be no acorns to make the hogs fat you had beter make beef of that cow for I no you will need her for you and the children for you cant fatten hogs with corn I no. Write soon and fail not and giv me the nuse. So I must close by saying I stil remain your affectionate husband tel death.

So fairwell Nancy C Yow.

William Henry Yow

My Dear Little Son[26]

I drop you a few lines in answer to your letter. Henry you said that you eat a heep of peaches. I expect you do and I do want to be their to eat peaches with you. You said that Bet and Walker had mended sinc you got them in the pasture. I am glad to here that tha hav mended. Do the best you can with your colt and you will hav to sel him this fall and I want you to get all you can for him. You must get your granpapy to help you sel him. He will do all he can for you. Henry you must be a good boy and be

Chapter Four

good to your mother and little brothers and sisters. May the good Lord bles and save you forever William Henry Yow. Matthew C Yow

Catharine Isaac and Jones is both well. Tha are on picket now. Tha will stay tel Saturday morning. I hop tha will hav good luck.

∽

Nancy Elisabeth Yow and Mary Jane Yow

My Dear Little Daughters[27]

I must drop you a few words in answer to your kind little letter. Nancy you said you was sick with the tooth ach. Pore little girl I am so sorrow for you. I hop you wil soon get wel and be harty. Nancy you must be a good girl and mind your mother. Mary Jane you said that you was rocking little Johny. That is rite Jane you must be a smart girl and mind your mother and be good to your little brothers. May the good Lord bles and sav my dear little children forever I pray.

Matthew C Yow to Nancy E Yow and Mary J Yow and Joseph G Yow and John M Yow my dear little sons and daughters. So fairwell for this time.

           M C Yow to Nancy E Yow.

∽

M. C. Yow
August the 21 1863

Catharine[28]

I will say to you that this day the 21 day of August was set apart for humiliation and prare.[29] We did not hav any duty to do at all. We read our Bibles and praid to the good Lord to help us in our troubles and bring peac on our distracted contry. O that the good Lord wold bring peac on our land and contry that we may return home to those that we love so well. Mr Reubin Manes[30] comes to our company and sings and prays with us. Reubin is just the same man yet our company thinks a heep of him. I do wish that he belong to our company for we hav no meeting at all only when he comes. He comes twice a week and prays with us. O, that the good Lord will here and answer our prares. We believ that you are all praying for us pore soldiers here in the army. I think this is a time that all ought to pray. But I fear that it is not don. O lord bles and sav us all I pray.

∼

M C Yow
August the 23

Catharine

    I wil tel you how tha do here. Friday the 21 was set apart for fasting and prare by Jef Davis and we had no duty to do that day and this the Sabbath the Lords day we hav to be rubing our guns and go out on inspection. That shoes to whos day tha respect the Lords day or Jef Davises day. I am afraid that it will be a bad chanc with some of our head men in time to come. I do wish tha wold try to do beter and I think we wold hav beter times than we do.[31]

M. C. Yow to Nancy C. Yow

∼

August the 24 1863

Chapter Four

Catharine
   I will to you again that I cant get no letters from my father. The last letter I got from him was dated July the 12 and non sinc. Your letters comes and I cant tel why his dont come. I do want to here from him and his family so bad. May the good (*Lord*) bles and sav you all forever I pray. Nancy C Yow

Taylorsville VA August the 30 63
Mrs Nancy C Yow

My Dear Wife
   I hav bin one more time permited to drop you a few lines to let you no that I am well at present truly hoping when this comes to hand it may find you and my dear little children well and harty. Catharine I hav not had no letter from you in 10 days. I am looking for a letter from you every mail. I receivd a letter from your father the 26 and I hav rote a letter to him to day. I cant get no letter from father yet. I cant tel what is the matter. I think he has rote to me but I cant get them. Catharine I will say to you that we hav left Fredricksburg and come to Taylorsville about 20 miles north of Richmond at the same plac wher we was when we went to Fredericksburg.
   Catharine I hav some hop that we are going to NC again soon and it may be that we shal go to Charlston. I dont much want to go their now but I want to go to NC. I am tired of Va but it seems like we cant get away from here. I haint got no news to rite to you of any importanc. From what I can here from NC tha will be bad times their. I herd that Lawhon's croud[32] had kild one man and he kild one of them. I herd a letter red to day from moor and it said that tha had a white flag up in fayatville NC and tha say tha will fight at home.

I Hope You Will All Remember Me

    Catharine I will send you 2 stamps and 2 fifty cents bills of mony and see if you get it. I hop you will. I cant rite much this time. Rite soon and fail not. I Stil remain your affectionate husband tel death parts us. So fairwell my dear wife Nancy C. Yow.

This letter dated August 23, 1863, shows Matthew's disgust concerning the use of the Sabbath Day to prepare for war after a day of prayer and fasting on August 21st. Matthew wrote, "That shoes to whoes day tha respect the Lords day or Jef Davises day." In this letter Matthew also complains about the mail system which he often found fault with (image courtesy of Larry R. Yow).

Image of Private Matthew C. Yow, Company D, Forty-eighth Regiment, North Carolina Troops. Image supplied by Ms. Thomas J. Cumby, North Carolina Troops, A Roster, 1861-1865, Volume XI, Infantry, 45th-48th Regiments, Raleigh: Division of Archives and History, 1987, pp. 363-364.

This image of Matthew C. Yow's commanding officers is found adjacent to his picture in Volume XI of North Carolina Troops 1861-1865: A Roster, *compiled by Weymouth T. Jordan, Jr. (courtesy of the State Archives of North Carolina). Pictured are (1) Colonel Samuel Hoey Walkup; (2) Major William Hogan Jones; (3) Captain William Henry Harrison Lawhon, Company D; (4) Adjutant John R. Winchester; and (5) Lieutenant John A. Thompson, Company G.*

This undated letter to Nancy and Mary Jane was written during the late summer of 1863. Nancy was reminded to be a good girl and mind her mother. Mary Jane's message from Papa was to be a smart girl, mind her mother, and be good to her little brothers (image courtesy of Larry R. Yow).

This undated letter to William Henry was written during the late summer of 1863. Matthew often exhorted his son, Henry, to be good as seen in this letter. In other letters, Matthew reminded Henry to obey his mother, read his book, feed his horse, and not to fight with his sisters (image courtesy of Larry R. Yow).

Image of Private Cornelius A. Stutts, Company D, Forty-eighth Regiment, North Carolina Troops. Image supplied by Fred McLeod, North Carolina Troops, A Roster, 1861-1865, Volume XI, Infantry, 45th-48th Regiments, Raleigh: Division of Archives and History, 1987, frontispiece. C. A. Stutts was married to Matthew's first cousin, Lydia Yow. He carved the rings that Matthew sent home to his wife and two daughters.

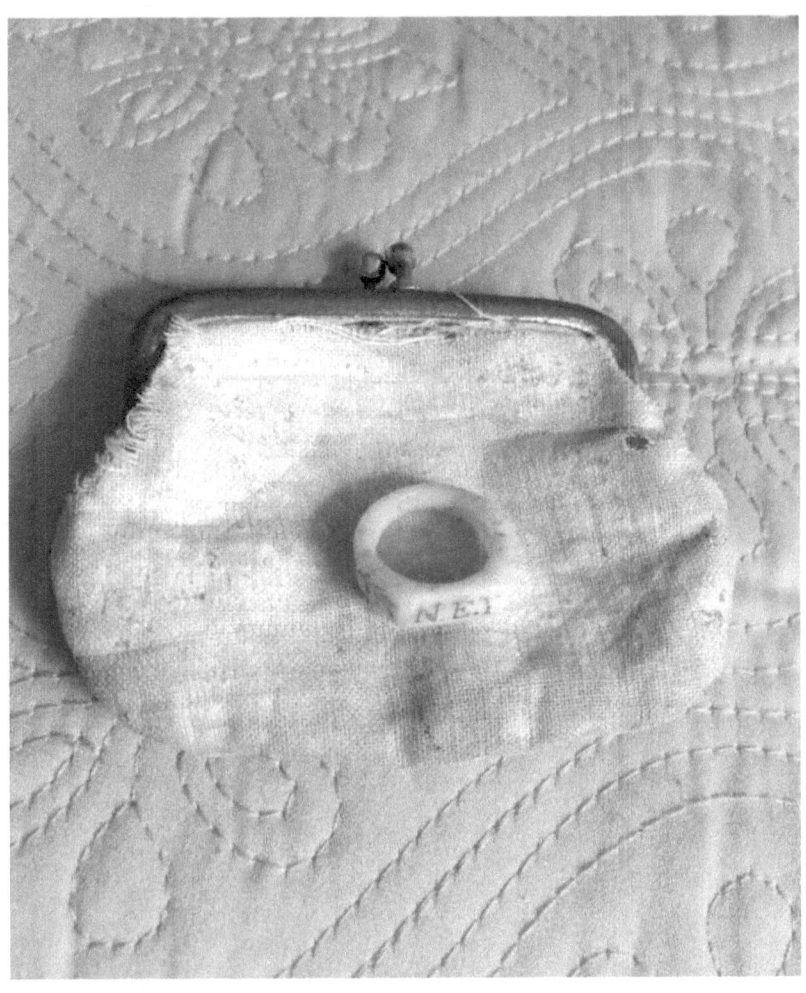

Matthew sent rings home to Catharine and their two daughters, Nancy and Mary Jane. Here is the one for Nancy engraved with her initials. Nancy's ring was given to this writer when she was a young girl with the instructions to pass it down to another Yow girl one day. That has been done. C. A. Stutts, one of Matthew's comrades in Co. D, made the rings and Matthew felt sure they would please the girls (image courtesy of Mark W. Yow).

This is a portion of a letter to Catharine and the children dated February 1, 1863. The letter is printed sideways to show how Matthew wrote the names of his children sideways across the top. He wrote, "William Henry Yow Nancy E Yow Mary J Yow Joseph G Yow John M Yow fairwell my dear little children may the lord bles and save you forever" (image courtesy of Larry R. Yow).

Entries of birth dates and wedding date for Matthew and Catharine Yow were recorded in Matthew's New Testament (image courtesy of Larry R. Yow).

June 17th 1863 . M.C. Yow
Mrs Nancy C. yow my dear wife and
little children Through the kind hand
of providence I hav bin spared to seat
myself to drop you a few lines to let
you no that I am well at present
duly hoping when this comes to hand
it may find you and the dear little
children well and harty Catharine
I hav not heard from you since I left
you at high point and I want to here
vary bad I am looking for a letter
from you now I hop I will get one
soon I wrote to you the day I got to
the company and I wrote to father since
and I thought I wold write to you also
to day and let you no where I am now
We are in camp about 11 miles East
of Richmond near the pines where
we fought the yankees last June
But I don't here any tel of a fight here
now I dont no what we come here for
But I suppose to wach for them

This is the first page of a letter sent to Catharine and the children dated June 17, 1863. This letter shows Matthew's best handwriting and has been better preserved than most of the other letters (Image courtesy of Larry R. Yow).

This second page of a letter sent to Joseph Albright was dated February 14, 1864. It was the most difficult letter to transcribe possibly because it was written in pencil and not well preserved. It was worth the effort to persevere in the task because this letter is quite interesting – it shows discord between Matthew and his father-in-law concerning the war and is the only letter that mentions General Robert E. Lee (image courtesy of Larry R. Yow).

poor little children it greavs hart to think that I cant come to them and tha are so near to my hart may god help you to keep them along rite and giv you helth to Work and pevide for them o that I cold see you and them one time more in this world may the good lord bles and giv you helth I pray So fairwell my dear Wife and little children

This is the last page of a partial undated letter sent to Catharine after the Battle of Bristoe Station in October 1863. Matthew, aware of his mortality, and worried about Catharine's health, shows much grief concerning the health and future of his children (image courtesy of Larry R. Yow).

Chapter Five
September 10 – November 20, 1863

"I no it takes a heep of money to get nothing now"

When Matthew left home to join the army in 1862, the Confederacy's problem of inflation had already started to spiral out of control. Matthew's early letters referenced the rising prices of many commodities such as apples, chickens, onions, and milk. In April 1862, he wrote to Catharine, "We cant get any thing with out paying double the worth." The reality was worse than that. "By the beginning of 1863 it took seven dollars to buy what a dollar had bought two years earlier."[1] The Confederate government struggled to finance the war and, in its efforts, subjected its citizens to unimaginable financial hardship.

On a meager military salary of eleven dollars a month, Matthew could not afford to splurge. He ate whatever the army rationed to him and saved as much as he could to send home to Catharine. Matthew could resist the temptation to eat exorbitantly priced sweets but he had to have his clothes washed once in a while. From Petersburg in August of 1862, he wrote that the price to have a shirt washed had risen from 5 cents to 15 cents, "and not half washt at that." He was also concerned about the rising costs of writing materials and stamps.

Catharine was barely able to keep the farm going and provide for her family. In the absence of Matthew and a suitable workforce, efficiency suffered. Production of corn and wheat was not adequate. One of her most urgent problems was keeping a supply of salt which was needed for meat preservation. It could be bought before the war for two dollars a bag, but by the fall of 1862 it was selling for 60 dollars a bag in some places.[2] Matthew often reminded Catharine to take good care of her salt. Catharine was probably very frugal and wise, but even the most disciplined housewife could not make ends meet in the economy of that time and place. It is understandable why the bread riots occurred in many large cities of the South in 1863 and why soldiers were choosing to desert from the ranks to go home and help their families.[3]

Catharine, alone in her home with five small children, was afraid at times. The war and all that resulted, the hunger and uncertainty, changed people. Matthew gave his wife advice on how to handle situations involving money because he knew Catharine and the children would suffer if it ran out or was stolen. He worried often about the situation in Moore and the surrounding counties; the runaway inflation and political climate played a part in how people treated each other. Even some neighbors could not be trusted.

The situation continued to get worse; the Confederate dollar in 1861 was worth 80 cents in gold and in 1865 it had devalued to 1.5 cents in gold.[4] There was a saying in the South during those difficult times, "...that a citizen went to market carrying his money in a basket and came home with the goods he had bought in his wallet."[5] In a letter to Catharine dated September 10, 1863, Matthew wrote, knowing the urgency of the times, "I dont

Chapter Five

think your neighbors will let you suffer as long as you hav money but when the money is gon it will be a bad chanc."

September the 10, 1863
Mrs Nancy C Yow

My Dear Wife

I seat myself to drop you a few lines to inform you that I am well at present truly hoping when this comes to hand it may find you and my dear little children well and harty. Catharine I rote a letter to you yesterday and I am going to drop you a few lines to send by Uncle John Stutts. He is going home on a furlo. I am going to send you some money. I will send you 25 dollars by him. I want to no how you are off for money now. Father said that you only draw (illegible) dollars[6] per month. I want to no what is the number that tha hav reducd your pay. It was little enoughf any how. Catharine I want you to send me one pair of socks by Uncle John. I haint got but one pair now and I dont no when we will draw any. Matthew C Yow

Catharine Uncle John says he will go to see you and I hop he will. Catharine the mail has come and no letter for me to day. The last letter I got from you was dated 21 of August and this is the 10 of September. That is a long time without hering from you and my dear little children. Catharine I am going to send you some money and I dont want you to tel any body that I sent it to you. For you no that their is some mean enoughf to take it from you and when you go to spend any dont show no more than you are going to spend. But you no who to sho your money to.

Catharine if your father wold buy the colt it wold be paying for the land. If you dont need the money your self and if you do need the money dont pay no dets. I want the dets paid but I dont want you to suffer for the money and I no your father dont want you to suffer by no means. But I hop you hav money enoughf to by any thing that you need. I think you ought to try to get you some salt before it gets so hi. I no it will get higher than it is now. I no it taks a heep of money to get nothing now. You said in your letter that you had to pay ten dollars for one bunch of thred. That does look hard and I dont think it is fair.

Catharine I hop Mr Moffitt[7] will be a good friend to you as he has bin. I no you will hav corn to by and I think you can get from him if you can get it from any body. I dont think your neighbors will let you suffer as long as you hav any money but when the money is gon it will be a bad chanc.

September the 17
Matthew C Yow to Nancy C Yow

Dear Wife and Little Children

A few more lines to you. I will send you this letter as I hav got it rote and you can read it and see what I was going to send to you by Uncle John Stutts. Catharine you said in one of your letters that you wanted me to send you a chew of my tobaco and I cold not think of it tel now and I will send it in this letter. Catharine I do want to here that peac is made so bad so that I and all thes pore soldiers can come home and sta with those that we lov so well and you that is always on our minds.

Catharine do the best you can for your self and the dear little children. Some times I study so much about them and what is to become of them. I cant hardly stand it to sta here. It is hard and I dont think it is fair. So I must close for this time. Rite as often as you can and maby I will get some of your letters. May god bles you is my prare. So fairwell. Mrs Nancy C Yow

Chapter Five

~

Taylorsville Station Va
M C Yow   September the 17 1863

Mrs Nancy C Yow my Dear Wife

I one time more seat my self to drop you a few lines to inform you that I am well at present truly hoping when this comes to hand it may find you and my dear little children well and harty. Catharine I will tel you that I am out of hart. I cant get no letters from you. The last I had from you was rote the 21 of August. I cant tel what is the matter. There is something rong some way. I cant tel whither you got my letters or not but I hop you do. Catharine when I cant here from you and the children I am out of hart for that is all the satisfaction that I can see is when I can here from you and here that you are all well and I think it is the same with you. Isaac and Jones dont get no letters and tha are out of hart as well as my self. Tha are both well exept bad cold Jones has. He cant hardly talk he is so horse and Isaac has a bad risen on his hand.

Catharine I can inform you that we hav a great meeting going on here now. It is a brigade meeting.[8] Their is a great prospect of doing a heep of good if we can sta here. Their has several profest (*professed*) now and the morners just goes in rouds.[9] I am so glad to see such good attention as is here now. Their is great revivals going on in the army at this time and their is a great need of it here. I hop you hav good meetings at home. This meeting is held by Mr Fairly[10] chaplin of the 27 Mr Howerton[11] of the 15 and Mr Dodson[12] of the 46. The 48 has no chaplin at this time. Its said that the Rev Mr Pliler[13] is coming to our regiment and I hop it is so. Catharine I rote a letter to send by Uncle John and he did not get off and I will send it in this as long as I hav got it rote. So no more for this time. I stil remain your true and affectionate husband tel death. So fairwell dear wife.

Taylorsville Station VA
September the 20 1863

Mrs Nancy C Yow my Dear Wife

    I am permitted to drop you a few lines to infom you that I am wel at present truly hoping when this comes to hand it may find you and my dear little children all wel and harty. Catharine I receivd 2 letters from you today one dated the 8 and the other 12 which made me so proud to here from you again. It has bin nearly three weeks sinc I had a letter from you and you no that I wanted to here from you and my dear little children. You said that Joseph had got well but John was sick now. I am so sorrow to here that he has the thrush so bad. Pore little children. I am so sorrow for them and I want to see them so bad. I am so uneasy about them. I am so afraid that tha wil tak that sore throat and if tha do I fear that it wil kil some of them.[14]

    You may no that I am in trouble. I study so much about you and them some times. It seems like I cant stand it much longer and I no that you are nearly scared to death sinc tha rob Brower. I dont no what will become of you all. You said that my pore old father was sick and had sent after the doctor and I no that he is bad off if he sent for the docter. I shant rest tel I here from him again. I got a letter from W N Brower the 18 and he said that father was sick and had sent for the docter and you said that some one had kild your sow and that made me vary mad when I red that. I no that it was old Hy Williamson for their is no body do that wold do that mean a trick but him and if I was their I wold try to make his back strait. I do hop and pray that I will get

Chapter Five

home again and I will help him kill my hogs. Any man that will such a trick as that will steal and I no he will do that. M C Yow

Catharine you said in one of your letters some time back that old Hy had kild my boar and I want to no if he did. It makes me so mad to think that any man will tak that mean a turn on you. but he noes that you cant help your self and I am gon now and I cant help my self but I cant my self now but I do hop I will get home again. It made me mad but I cant help it now. Such men as him wants you and your little children to suffer but I hop you will not. I suppose that ---- is dead and their is no body dead he was not fit to die nor fit to liv without he had ----. Catharine you said that Wesley Brower had offerd you 75 dollars for the colt. I think you can get one hundred dollars for him. Get all you can and then old Hy will come and steal the money from you. He is mean enough to do it I no. Do the best you can. M C Yow

Catharine all is quiet here now. I dont here much tel of fiting about here. I hop tha wont be much more don in Va. You said you thought that we ought to come home and defend our homes and I think so two. We want to come and kil them all when we here how tha are doing their. It is hard to bear. You said that you was sorrow that me and your father cold not agree. He is all rite. He dont make me mad. He thinks that he nows all about the war but he is mistaken. He can read the papers but tha dont tel the truth. Tha talk to incourage the soldiers. Holden[15] talks to suit me and all the soldiers is for him and Govener Vanc[16] and old Sam Christian.[17] We say baby for Sam. Catharine my dear wife rite soon so no more at this time. May God bles you all. So fairwell.

81

I Hope You Will All Remember Me

September the 28 63

Catharine

We hav good meeting here yet we had to move but we hav commenct here again. I herd 2 sermonds preacht yesterday and a great many morners. Tha will be some Baptists here to day and preaching again to nite. It seems like the good Lord is working a mong his people now. I am so glad to see and here of so much good being don not only here but all through the Confederate army. I believ that we cold do more good by praying for peac than we cold do by fiting for peac. If we hav to fight for peac we shant hav it soon. I do hop that something will soon be don. Catharine I rote to your father and he did not answer me. I dont no what is the matter. I hop I did not make him mad. When I rote to him last I rote plain and he does the same. It all goes rite with me. I am glad to here from him and here what he thinks about this cruel war. It is so bad. M C Yow

Catharine I rote a letter to you the 24 about selling the colt. You said in your letter that you did not think that you cold get more than 80 dollars for him and Mr wright[18] said that he wold giv 90 dollars for him without seeing him. He said he newd his mother and I rot to you to let his son James[19] hav him if you cant do any beter. He said tha wold pay you 60 dollars their and he wold pay me 30 dollars here and I hop you hav got the letter. We both rote a letter the same time and sent them. Catharine maby I can get to send the money to you before you need it. Do the best you can and get some wheet sowd if you can. Catharine my dear wife I do want to see you so bad and my dear little children. Catharine Jones says I look the best he ever saw me. I weigh one hundred and 50 pounds. So no more for this time. May God bles all. So fairwell my dear wife Nancy C Yow

Chapter Five

October the 11 1863
Gordonsville VA

Mrs Nancy C Yow my Dear Wife

    I one time more seat myself to drop you a few lines to inform you that I am well at present and I do hop and trust when this comes to hand it may find you and my dear little children all well and harty. Catharine I receivd your welcome letter to day that you rote the 27. It come to hand in due time. I hav bin geting letters regular for the last 2 weeks. You say that you get my letters regular. I am glad to here that you get my letters. I write vary often to you. No body do not write to me but you. My father cant rite to me.

    Catharine I will say to you that your brother John come to see me yesterday and he staid with me half of the night. He come here to get one of there guns brusht and he left here this morning. Henry was well and also John Rich[20]. John looks well but he is like myself. He is tiard of the war. He told me how Thomas Craven[21] treated him when he went home. I allways thought that Tom was mean and now you can tel what he will do. He is one of the tories. I reckon Coffin and Dorset is the same way.[22] For he will do as tha do you no. John come to see me and he wanted to see Isacc and Jones and we went to see them and staid a long time and talk with them. Jones had such a bad cold that he cold not talk only whisper but he is some beter today.

    Catharine you said that you went to Mr Moffitt to get corn and did not see him. I think he will let you hav corn. You tel him that I said he must let you hav corn if he let any body hav any and I no that he will hav corn to sell. You said that you hav 2 hogs in the pen and tha was fat. That is the way for you to do. Keep some always in the pen if old Hy dont kill them all. He is mean enough to kill you and tak your money.

    Catharine dont let any body no that you hav much money. I

expect you hav a good eal of money now and when you sel the colt you will hav more. I reckon you hav got my letter that I rote to you about the colt. Mr rite wants him vary bad and I am afraid that you cant feed what you will hav left. I am vary uneasy about you. I am afraid that you will suffer yet it greavs my hart that I cant be their to make somthing for you and my dear little kids to live on. I do hop and pray that their will be ----. May god help you to rais my dear children. Catharine dont forget me in your prares. I believ you do pray for me. I am always praying for you and my dear little children and my dear sick father. I hop he will bear his sickness with patience. May God bles and rais him up.

Catharine I expect that I will hav to go into another battle before long. I think tha will be sure to fight on the Rappadan River. We are in 15 miles of that place. Johns camp is on the bank of the river. The Yankees on one side and our men on the other. If I do hav to go into battle with them I pray to the good Lord to be with me there and save me from all danger. Catharine from what I can here their is bad chanc at home now. I suppose tha are kiling some and sending some to the army. Tha go along here every day.[23] Catharine giv lov and best respects to all my friends. Tel my old granfather that I hav not forgot him yet. I do want to see him and all the rest of you so bad I cant hardly stand it. So I must close for this time. I remain your affectionate husband tel death. M C Yow Fairwell to Nancy C Yow

October the 18 1863 M. C. Yow

Mrs Nancy C. Yow my Dear Wife

I do thank my God that I hav one more opportunity of riting you a few lines one time more. I will say to you that I am well as I cold expect at this time. We hav bin marching 10 days and fiting

Chapter Five

together. Wensday the 14 we had a fight at Bristo Station[24] 4 miles this side of Manasses Gap. I did not get hurt much. A ball hit me on the thigh but did not go through my cloths but I hav bad news to tel you. My Brother Simeon J Yow is I fear mortaly wonded. He was shot through the left brest and the ball went out under the left shoulder blade. I do hop it will not kil him. I went to see him next day and he lookt vary bad but he said that it did not hurt him vary bad. He dont think that it will kil him. He was shot through the left hand also pore fellow. I am so sorrow for him. He was a good soldier. He was pushing on the Yankees when tha shot him. His captain hast it vary bad for he was such a good soldier. Isaac was hurt some. He is with Jones or was at last account. Isaac was not hurt so bad but what he cold take care of Jones. The yankees repulst us one time but we held the battle field and tha left that night and went to Manasses and we did not follow them. Some followed them and fought them next day and drove them on.

Catharine I cant rite much this time. We shal hav to march vary soon now. We are at the Rappahanoc River a wating to cros. It has raind so much that the river is vary high. We hav bin tearing up the railrode for the last 2 days. We are coming back as fast as we can. We aim to get to Culpeper today if we can cros the River. Catharine I hav seen hard times for the last 10 days. Your brothers was in the fight but did not get hurt. I think I will get some letters from you now. We haint had no mail in 10 days. It cold not get to us. I got a letter from W N Brower the day I left Gordonsville but I cold not answer it then. We had one man kild in our company and several wonded and 10 taken prisnors. Levi Right was taken prisnor.

Catharine I will rite as soon as I stop and tel you more about the times here. Tel my father that I will rite to him soon as I can. I dont want him to greav so much about my dear brother. I do hop that he will get well. Jones is sent to Culpeper now. I want to see him when I get their. Jones was rite pert yesterday. Tha said that he cold walk a little. I am nearly brok down. My feet is all over blisters but I keep going yet. So I must close for this time. I will rite again as soon as I can. May God bles you all I pray. Catharine do the best you can. Write as often as you can. Fairwell.

Matthew C Yow Nancy C Yow

Catharine [25]

I am glad that William met with Horner.[26] He giv more than Shaw[27] would giv and more than Write wold giv. Write[28] Was taken prisnor. He has gon to sta with the yankees awhile now. Catharine do the best you can and get corn as cheap as you can. I am so uneasy about you now. I thought you had got well. If you get sick I donot no what will becom of our little children. Pore little children. It greavs hart to think that I cant come to them and tha are so near to my hart. May God help you to keep them along rite and giv you helth to work and provide for them. O that I cold see you and them one time more in this world. May the good Lord bles and giv you helth I pray. So fairwell my dear wife and little children.

M. C. Yow to Nancy C Yow

October the 23 1863

Mr Joseph Albright Dear Father

Through the kind hand of Providenc I am permited one time more to drop you a few lines to inform you that I am well at

Chapter Five

present truly hoping when these lines reaches you tha may find you and family enjoying good helth. I receivd your letter the 6 which come to hand in due time and was truly glad to here that you was all well. I hav not had the chanc to answer your letter tel now. We got marching orders the 8 and the 9 we left Gordonsville and the 6 day we over took the enemy at Bristo Station near Manasses. At about 2 oclock we opend fire on them. Grahams Battry[29] opend the fire and it was a close time for a while. The enemy was hid behind the railrod and we cold not see them and we had no protection at all and the Yankee batteries was playing on us all the time.[30] It was said that tha had 40 peaces. You may be sure that tha opend our ranks. Tha repulst one time but we held the battle field and lay their that night and the cowardly Yankees left under cover of night. Next morning tha was all gon. Tha was followed by our cavalry. We lost one man kild and 10 wonded one mortaly wonded and 10 taken prisners.[31] We lost 700 and 75 men out of the brigade. That was a bad loss for the time that we was their.[32]

It is said that it was badly managed and I think so myself. I am afraid that General Heath[33] is not a good commander. Them that has bin under him say that he is not successful. General Cook was badly wonded. I herd that he was ded but I think it as a mistake. His leg has bin taken off.[34] I suppose Colonel Hall[35] is in command now. Henry and John was not hurt. I saw John next day. My 2 brothers was both wonded. Jones was badly wonded I am afraid mortaly but I hop not. He was shot through the left brest and the ball come out under the left shoulder blade and he was shot through the left hand.

I am vary sorrow for him. He was a good soldier. His captain hats it vary bad. He thought a heep of Jones and Isaac. Isaac was slitly wonded by a shel. He will soon be able for duty I think. I was hit on the thigh but the ball did not go through my cloths. We are on the south side of the Rappahanoc River. I cant tel how long we shal sta here. I got a letter from Catharine the 20 and she said that she was not well. She said that she had bin to the doctor again. I fear that she will get down sick yet. So no more. Your friend tel death.

M. C. Yow   Joseph Albright

October the 25 1863

Mrs Nancy C Yow my Dear Wife

With pleasure I seat my self to drop you a few lines inform you that I am well at this present time and I do trust when this comes to hand it may find you and my dear little children all well and harty. Catharine I hav not had no letter from you in several days but I am looking for a letter now and I thought I wold to you to day. It seems like I cant be satisfied with I am riting to you. I think that you want to here from me and I no I want to here from you as often as I can. I dont see anything but trouble now. My brother is so badly wonded and I cant here from him and I am so uneasy about you and the children that I dont see any satisfaction at all. I can here how things is going on about home and it greavs me for I no if this war last much longer you will suffer.

The wether is geting cold and I study so much about you and pore little Henry. I dont no what you will do this winter and I see no chanc for me to come home to help you. O that the good Lord wold giv us peac one time more in this distracted country. I hav prayd for peac all the time and there is thousands of prares going up every day for peac and it seems to do no good. But I do thank my God that I am aliv and doing as well as I am. I am well and harty if I cold get enough to eat but I dont get enough but I dont mind that. I will freely suffer my self but I cant bear to

Chapter Five

think of you and my dear little children suffering. But it seems like their is no other chanc for you. Every thing is so clear that your money will not hold out long I am afraid. Do the best you can. May god help you I pray. God bles my dear little children I pray.

~

November the 19 1863

Mrs Nancy C Yow Dear Wife

    I am truly thankful that I am one time more permited to drop you a few lines to inform you that I am well at this present time and I do hop when this letter reaches you it may find you and my dear little children wel and harty. Catharine I receivd your letter of the 9 the 15. I did not rite when I got your letter. I had just rote one to you the same day before I got yours. I was so glad to here from you all. I was sorrow to here that little Nancy was so bad off with the toothache. I hav had a hard spel of the toothach my self. It is bad I no. Catharine you said that you was troubled so bad about me not geting enough to eat. I dont want you to think much about that. I can bear that. I dont mind it for myself as bad as I do for you and my little children. That is what greavs me so bad to think that you hav to giv so much for corn and I am here fiting for them that you get corn from as wel as for myself. It looks hard for them to charg you so much and if tha wold consider the case tha wold not do so. Our people has got two hard harted to do the thing that is rite. It looks hard and I dont think it is fair. You said that Columbus[36] was plowing for you yet and he got along mity slow. I do hop you can get your wheat sowd. I am afraid that your ground is not in good fix to sow. Maby it will make some wheat. Matthew C. Yow

    Catharine you said that you had 4 hogs up and I am afraid

that you cant get corn to make them fat. It will be a pity to kil them half fat. I fear that you will hav to do it. May God help you to provide for our dear little children. O that I cold see them now. I do want to see you all so bad. May God bles you I pray. Catharine Jones will be at home before this letter gets their if he has good luck. I hop he will get home safe. I cant tel you when I can come to see you again. I fear it will be a long time if ever. I hop that my life will be spard to get through this cruel war and get home again but it looks like a bad chanc now but I hop it will get beter soon. But the prospect looks vary gloomy at this time tho it may soon close. I hop it may.

I fear we shal have a hard battle here yet and I fear it will be soon tho it may not be. I hop it may not. Catharine I dont no what to rite to you. I hav nothing good to rite. I want you to rite to me as often as you can and let me no how you are geting along. I rote to your father and I got no answer from him. I dont no why he dont rite to me. I hav not seen your brothers sinc the battle at Bristo. Tha are not far from here. We are on the Rappadan River yet and we shal sta here tel the Yankees makes some move. I am looking for a letter from you and father now. Tel Jones when he gets home to rite to me. So I will close for this time by saying I stil remain your affectionate husband tel death. So fairwell my dear wife Nancy C Yow.

November the 20 1863

Catharine the mail come last night and no letter for me. I will send this off this morning. I hav no stamps to put on my letters but I hop you can pay the postag and if you want to here from me as bad as I want here from you you will pay it freely. Catharine I am wel this morning. I hop this may find you wel. Catharine I dream so much about being at home. I hop I will get home before long. I was with you all night last I saw you and the

Chapter Five

children as plain as I ever did in my life but when I awakd I was not with you. I cant help but study about my dream. Matthew C Yow to Nancy C Yow May God bles you I pray.

 Catharine giv my lov to my brothers and sisters. You said that Sarah[37] was vary bad off. I am sorrow to here that for I expect it is hard times with them now as wel as your self. Tel father that I will rite to him before long. I want him to rite to me as often as he can and giv me the news. From what I can here their is bad times in Moor County. Tha are hunting and eating up every thing. It is a bad chanc I think any how. So fairwell.

Catharine [38]

I hav no news of interest to rite to you only we hav got to our winter quarters at last. We hav built us huts to sta in and hav chimneys to them. We are about 3 miles east of Orang C H So I must close for this time. Write as often as you can. I stil remain your affectionate husband tel death.
M. C. Yow to Nancy C. Yow

Tel Jones that I said not to come here tel he ---- and well.[39] I want to see him as bad as I can but I dont want him to come here tel he gets well. I praid to the good (Lord) for him to recover and I do hop he will. Tel him for my sake not to forget to pray for himself. Catharine I am praing for you all and I hop that my prare will be answered. I do hop and pray that soon be made but I ---- expect at this time for it ---- for it to come ---- Isaac I rote to ---- not answered ---- hop that he has gone ---- Catharine I rote to you to something when to eat if he can bring it. I want something from home. Wold eat so good to me. I do want to come to see you so bad but I cant tel when I can.

Catharine giv my best respects to all my brothers and sisters and all my friends ---- If any tel them all that I hav not forgoten them yet. You said that the hunters[40] had shot Georg Moore[41] and John Williamson.[42] I recon that some is glad that Georg is dead. I no their is bad times their now but I hop tha will not pester you non. Nothing that you hav got dont let no body cheat ---- of any thing that you ------ I hop that father will ---- and help you to ----.

Catharine as soon as you can me no how you are so I must close by saying I stil remain your husband tel death parts us. M. C. Yow

Nancy C. Yow Fairwell.

Chapter Six
January 5 – April 4, 1864

"For he has his opinion and I hav mine"

When the war began in April 1861, people had to affirm their loyalty to one side or the other and sometimes men in the same family chose different sides. An example of this is the family of Matthew's brigadier general, John Rogers Cooke. Cooke chose to fight for the Confederacy while his father, General Phillip St. George Cooke, remained loyal to the Union army.[1] Two of J. R. Cooke's three sisters married well-known Confederates and one married a Union general. His sister, Flora, married the Confederate cavalryman, Jeb Stuart. The situation was not so extreme in the Yow and Albright families; they stayed loyal to the Southern cause. However, they had differences of opinion about the new government and its leaders that threatened to undo their civility toward each other.

In these letters, we see a rift continuing between Matthew and his father-in-law, Joseph Albright. This is first seen in a letter to Catharine dated September 20, 1863, in which

Matthew replied to her concern about him not agreeing with her father. He wrote, "He is all rite. He dont make me mad." Matthew knew that Catharine's father read the newspapers, most of which were partisan; he thought Mr. Albright's perception of the war was misguided by what he read.

The morale of many North Carolinians was at its lowest as the end of 1863 approached. Life was hard for women trying to manage farms and households without their husbands. Many soldiers had become weary and could no longer see a way to win the war. The devastating losses at Gettysburg and Vicksburg removed the last vestige of hope from many minds that Southern victory would come. At this point, some just wanted peace on any terms.

Governor Vance was challenged as he tried to lead perhaps the most politically diverse people of the Confederate states. Not only was there tension within the state, but also between the state and the Confederate government. Many issues including conscription and tax-in-kind laws, civil liberties, and the suspension of the writ of habeas corpus gave impetus to the protest meetings that were occurring in many places throughout the state. This resistance to the Confederate government began to gain much popularity under the leadership of William W. Holden, the editor of the *North Carolina Standard*. Holden challenged Vance for the governorship in 1864 and ran his campaign on the peace movement that grew out of the anti-government protests. Two men with different visions of how to obtain peace and thousands of people arguing about the best man to choose characterized the times. Vance believed peace could be obtained only by continuing the fight until independence from the Union was assured. Holden, on the other hand, wanted to obtain peace through a reunification with the North, thus preventing more bloodshed.

The winter and spring of 1864 brought campaign speeches

Chapter Six

at home and in the army. Before the gubernatorial vote would occur in August many citizens would debate the best choice for North Carolina's future. In these letters, we see Matthew at odds with his father-in-law about the issues of their day. Matthew, hurt by Mr. Albright's accusation of his disloyalty to the cause, assured his father-in-law that he was as loyal as any man; he hoped to see independence, but he didn't want to fight anymore. In his letter to Joseph Albright in this chapter, we see Matthew being respectful to his wife's father despite their differing opinions. Matthew and Mr. Albright mutually agreed through their correspondence to not talk about politics going forward. They came to realize that to keep peace in the family they should hereafter talk only about the health of the family.

January 5 1864   Matthew C. Yow

Dear Wife and Little Children

I one time more seat my self to drop you a few lines which will inform you that I am as well as I cold expect for what I hav bin through with. I was on picket the first day of January and it was the coldest day that I ever saw. I thought I should freez but I did not quite. Catharine I do hop when this reaches you it may find you all well. I am going to send this by ---- Pool.[2] I Will send Henry 14 buttons and you a half pound of soda. She said that she would go to see you and tel you that she seed me. Catharine I wanted to send you somthing but I did not no what elc to send to you. I paid two dollars and 50 cents for the soda and one dollar for the buttons. The wether is vary cold. It is snowing now and it looks like we shal all freez. Mrs. Nancy C Yow

Catharine tha hav a new post offic at Richmond and I will tel you how to direct your letters Matthew C. Yow Co. D. 48 Regiment N C Troops Cooks Brigade A N VA. This means the Army of Northern Virginia. Tha say that the letters will come quicker and better to us. Catharine I am riting this to send by Mrs Pool. I dont no when she will leav here. I thought I wold rite to day. I may be off on picket when she leaves. I am looking for a letter from you and father now. It has bin snowing all day. I fear tha will be a deep snow here and it will be a bad chanc here. Wood is so scearc here. Catharine I study a heep about you. This wether may God help to get along and hav good luck. I no you see hard times and I am so sorrow for (*you*). May God bles you all is my prare. So fairwell Nancy C Yow

January the 16 1864

Dear Wife and Little Children

I do thank the Lord that I am one time more permited to drop you a few lines which will inform you that I am well and I do hop and trust when this reaches you it may find you all well and harty. Catharine I receivd your vary welcom letter last night the 15 that you rote the 6. It has bin a long time on the way. I was so glad to here from you for it had bin a long time sinc I had a letter from you. I was vary sorrow to here that little John was sick. I do hop that he is not dangerous. Catharine you said that you see so much trouble. I no it is hard to bear but try to bear it the best you can. I hav rote several letters to you that I hav not herd from. I sent 50 cents in one to Henry and 50 cent bills and some stamps for another to you and I fear you did not get them as you do not mention them.

Catharine James Hunsucker[3] came back last night and he told a big tail. He told me that W. N. Brower told him that Dorcas[4] went to Carters[5] and she was bearfooted and she told

Chapter Six

Carter that she did not hav any bred in the hous and he said Matthews family was in the same fix. I told him that was a lie or you did not write the truth to me and I did not think that you wold do that. But I did not thank him for his news for I did not believ that was so.

Catharine I hav sent you some money this morning by Mr Reubin Maness. I expect you will get the money before this letter comes to hand. Catharine I sent you 10 dollars. I cold hav sent you some moore but I may need it here. I think I shal get to come to see you this spring. There is 4 men gon from our company now. You said that Joseph sais he wants papy to come home. Pore little children. When I red that the tears dropt from my eys. Catharine I am sorrow to here that you had such bad luck with your cows. I am afraid that you cant get feed for them this winter. Do the best you can. You said that Columbus was haling hay. Then I do hop you can get feed. You said that Moffit said he cold not let you hav corn much longer. I do hop you can get corn some where. I thought that W. N. Brower was going to let you hav corn. I hav rote to him and I recon he is ashamed to rite to me sinc he told you about the corn and bread. I hop the good Lord will help you so no more at present.

M. C. Yow to Nancy C. Yow

January the 27 1864

Mrs Nancy C Yow Dear wife

Through the mercies of our heavenly (Father) I am one time moore permited to drop you a few lines which will inform you that I am well at this present time truly hoping when this reaches you it may find you and the dear little children all well and harty. You said in your letter which I receivd the 25 that you rote the 20 that the children had vary bad colds. That is vary common here. I hop that the dear little children will get well before this comes to hand. Catharine I am glad to here that you got the money that I sent by Reubin Maness and the soda that I sent by Mrs Pool. She told (*me*) that she wold go to see you and take the things to you and I suppose she did and she told you that I was so fat and pretty. I am vary fleshy now and I feel well and I am vary harty. But I cant get enough to eat here. But it may be the best for me not to hav enough to eat here. Catharine I never saw so many baskets as come here now. Tha come by the hundreds from home to the soldiers. But you liv so far from the railrode that you cant send me any thing to eat.[6]

Catharine Big John Crisco[7] come to see me yesterday. It supprised me to see him here. I thought I wold (*send*) this letter by him but I was on gard and did not hav the chanc to rite. Catharine I come in time to see a bad site. Their was a man shot here yesterday.[8] He belong to the 48 Regiment Co. K from Forsyth County and their will be 3 shot next Saturday. Tha belong to the 46 N C Regiment. If I liv tel then I shal hav to see them shot and it is a bad looking sight to see. Men had beter not runaway than to hav to be shot to death. I dont want my brothers to sta at home after their furlows are out or tha cant get them extended any longer. If tha do tha will be taken up in Richmond. Every man that come through there and his furlow is out tha take him up. I am looking for 3 letters from Jones and I think that I will soon. We haint movd from this camp yet. I suppose we will next week if nothing happens.

Catharine you said that little Joseph wants his pap to come home so he can sit in his lap. Bles his dear little soul. I do want to see you all so bad. Father said in his letter that little John M has bin sick and he went to see Doctor Shaw[9] and paid one dollar for medicine for him. Catharine you said that you were going to send me something good to eat by Jones when he comes. I wold be more than glad to get something to eat from him if you can spare it without taking somthing from the children that tha need and I dont want you to do that. I do want to get to come home and eat some good food with you and Betsy.[10] I expect you both hav some that is good. Catharine we hav nice wether here now. For the last 4 days it looks like spring. I told Uncle John today that you was planting your onions and peas if the wether was as pretty there as it is here. I no it cant sta so here long in these mountains. You said that you wanted me to come home to see your new garden. I will if I can and I hop I will get to come in March or April if not before.

Catharine I do want to see you ----. It has bin most 7 months sinc I saw you. Lord send that happy time when we shal meet again. Some times I cant think that this war can last much longer but if it does last tel next summer their will be the hardest fiting don that ever has bin don yet. But I do hop and pray that it will be stopt by March. If it dont we will all perish here and at home two. Catharine you said that your father was mistaken when he rote to me that you was in good hart. I new that wold not do. He allways tries to incourage me. I rote him a plain letter. I dont no what he will think and I dont much care. I dont like to here men speak up for this cruel war when I no that it is not just or I dont think it is. Catharine you never told whither Columbus was going to make a crop for you or not. I rote to you to let him in at his offer. You said that he wold work for one third of the crop and I expect that is the best chanc you will get. Let me no in your next letter. In conclusion I will to you to pray for me. I stil remain your affectionate husband tel death.

Matthew C Yow to Nancy C Yow

I Hope You Will All Remember Me

~

February the 14 the 15 1864[11]

Father and Family

With ----seat my self to drop----lines which will----that I am well ----present time truly hoping this----you all well and harty. I received your letter in due time----suprised me vary much the way you rote to me you must think that I am a disloyal man----to my country at all----you must think that I had some notion of going to the Yankees by sending me the Abalishion Oath[12]. I care nothing about that oath. I expect that me and you will hav to take that oath yet without----what tha are at.

You said that I was like some of my disrespected neighbors ... like to hav the disrespect----throwd up to me that I----and I no that I hav----as well as any----feelings to think that you thought such a thing as that about me just because I rote to you that I was out of hart. I am out of hart and I dont see any thing to put me in hart for what little money we get is no----it wont by any thing hardly at all. You said the army rations was small. Tha seem not to agree with me. I hav a good part of them to by or I should suffer. You say that provisions is plenty. I dont see why we dont get it. General Lee sais that tha hav ----every exertion that tha can----cant get it and he dont----on that account----that we must trust in God...[13]

If you go to the Bible about this war I can tel you that it sais their shal be no Confederacy.[14] I want to no what you think of that. You said somthing about the Revolution. If I knowd that we had the ----that tha had I could be in beter hart.[15] But I ----think so it looks two much like----people but this----as for my part I am tired of this war and I want it to stop and I dont much care how...

I hop and believe that the good Lord will take care of you. So

Chapter Six

I will close my letter by saying I stil remain your affectionate son tel death.

       Matthew C Yow to Joseph Albright

~

March the 7 1864

Mrs Nancy C Yow Dear Wife

 I this beautiful morning seat my self to drop you a few lines which will inform you that I am blest with tolerable good helth and I do hop and trust when this reaches you it may find you and my dear little children all wel and doing wel. Catharine I receivd your welcom letter the 4 that you rote the 28. I also receivd one from father the same time.

 Catharine I was so glad to here that you was all wel. Catharine I rote a letter to you the 3 and one to father the 4 before I got your letters. Tel father that I will rite to him soon. Jones got here last Sunday the 3. I was so glad to see him and I was sorrow two. He looks mity wel. Catharine it hurt my feelings vary bad to here how he don while at home. Father told me all about him in his letter. I do hate it vary much. He cant get any thing to drink here. Catharine tomorrow the 8 is a day set apart for fasting and prare. I hop that day will be holy.

 All is quiet here now. The wether has bin so bad that the Yankees could not do any thing. I expect that we shal hav bad times here this spring. I do dredit. I do hop that the good Lord will spare my life And take me through safe. Catharine do the best you can and pray for me that I may be savd from the hands of my enemies. So I will close by saying I stil remain your affectionate husband tel death.

       M. C. Yow to Nancy C. Yow

I Hope You Will All Remember Me

~

March the 12 1864
Camp near Orang C H VA

Mrs Nancy C Yow Dear Wife

I hav bin one time more permited to drop you a few lines which will inform you that I am wel at present and I do hop when this reaches you it may find you and my dear little children all wel and doing wel. Catharine I receivd your kind and welcome letter the 9 that you rote the 3. I was so glad to here that you and the children was wel for that is all the pleasure that I can see is when I can here that you are all wel. Catharine I dont see much satisfaction here but I no that it wont do to giv up. I try to do the best I can. I read a great deal in the Bible. I read the good promises of them that is faithful.

Catharine I will say to you that John Manes has got to the army at last. He was attacht to the 27 regiment Co A. We are close to gether now. Jones has come but you no that before now he is wel as common he has a caugh. He has rote to you Catharine. I want to no how him and Youtha[16] was geting on when he was at home. I never said any thing to him about it. He told me that he staid their the night that he left home. Catharine you don rite when you would not let Columbus work for you when he began to tryout. I dont want any of the deserters to sta about you. Tha had as wel come here as me.[17]

Catharine it seems lik your father wants to incourage me so much to sta and do my duty he would do more for you than he does. I dont get mad with him for riting as he does for he has his opinion and I hav mine. He sais he has rote to incourage me but he should quit and just rite about the helth of the family. Catharine do the best you can for I see no chanc to get to come home this spring. I do hate it so bad. I expect we shal hav bad

Chapter Six

times here before long. Tha are fixing every thing for to be ready to march at any time. The wether has bin so bad that tha could not move any way. As soon as the wether brakes tha will be somthing don. Catharine you may no that I do dred what I think will come on this spring but I will do the best I can and trust in the good Lord that has brought me though many dangers.

Catharine you said that you was glad that I could send you paper. I will send you all that I can. I will send you some in this letter. I sent you some coffee and sugar by Uncle John. I hop that you got it all. You said you wanted me to use it. I am using what I got now. Catharine rite as often as you can and let me no how you are geting along. Jones sais that Henry can plow. I hop that you can make somthing this year. May God help you I pray. Tel Isaac to rite to me and let me no how he is geting along. Catharine if I never should see you any more in this world I hop that we will meet in haven where we shal part no more. So I must close by saying I stil remain your affectionate husband tel death.

M C Yow to Nancy C Yow

~

April the 4 1864
Camp near Orang C. H. VA

Mr Joseph Albright Dear Father and Family

Through the mercies of our heavenly (*Father*) I hav bin one time more permited to drop you a few lines which will inform you that I am not in as good helth as I hav bin. I hav had a hard spel of thoothach and sore throat which hurt me vary bad. But I am now on the mend truly hoping when this reaches you it may find you all wel and doing wel. I receivd your letter some days back. I was truly to hear that you was all wel. The reason I didnot write no sooner I was not wel. Their is a good many sick here now and I dont no what is the caus. Some say that it is the water.[18] I cant tel the caus of it. You rote me a long letter and it seems like from the way you write that you think that I hav no confidenc in you but you are mistaken. I ask your appinion and you giv it and I dont think hard of you for that. I will agree with you. I believ you are candid in what you say and I think you believ what you write and I do hop that it will come to pass that we may gain our independenc and be a free and happy people one time more. I believ that I am as true to my country as you or any other man but I am like a great many others. I hav becom tired of this war and some times I get out of hart and then I dont care how it goes so I can hav peac. Peac is what I want but I want it on fare terms and I dont want to fight any more. The more we fight the more we may fight.

Govner Vanc come to see us and made a long speech. He sais that we must fight them tel hell freezes over.[19] I call that a drab expression. I didnot like that at all. He is a great man if he was not so wicked. It seems that the most of our ruling men is wicked men and I believ that hurts our caus. All things will come rite some day and I hop it is not far distant. I didnot rite to you to insult you at all and if you rote to me to insult me you did not. You said you would not write any thing here after only about the health of your family. It all will be rite with me. My Lieutenant Cleg[20] red the letter that you rote to me and he said that it was the best letter that he had seen sinc he had bin in the servis. He sais that ----hart.

H. A. Albright come to see me the other day. He was wel and he said that John was wel. All is quiet here now but I cant tel what a day may bring forth. The wether has bin vary bad for some time. Pleas giv my lov and best respects to all my friends. So I must close. Rite soon and fail not.

Chapter Six

Your friend tel death.
Matthew C Yow   Joseph Albright

This is the third page of the last letter in this collection and is dated April 4, 1864. Matthew wrote this letter to his father-in-law, Joseph Albright. He made it clear that he was tired of the war and did not want to fight anymore. He also wrote about his disappointment in Governor Vance's speech when he visited the brigades of Cooke and Kirkland the previous week (image courtesy of Larry R. Yow).

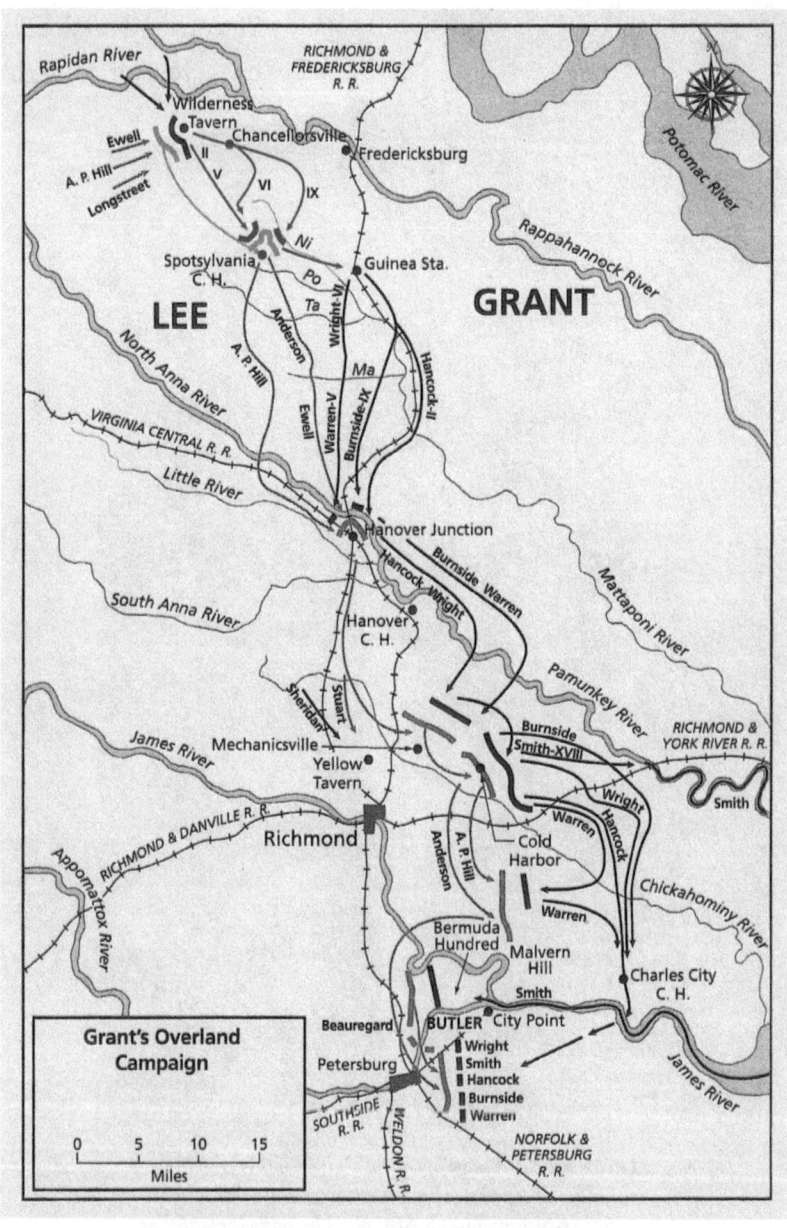

Map of the Overland Campaign from *Bloody Spring* by Joseph Wheelan, copyright © 2014. Reprinted by permission of Da Capo Press, an imprint of Hachette Book Group, Inc.

Chapter Seven
April, 1864 – April, 1865

"All is quiet here now but I cant tel what a day may bring forth"

The fourth day of April in 1864 was dreary and cold for Matthew and his comrades camped near Orange Court House, Virginia. Snow, rain, and sleet fell from the gray sky; the wind howled and blustered around the mud huts.[1] It was on this day that Matthew penned a letter to Joseph Albright, his father-in-law, that became the last of Catharine's treasured collection. He wrote that he was tired of the war, did not want to fight anymore, and wanted peace on fair terms. In closing the letter, he wrote, "All is quiet here now but I cant tel what a day may bring forth." This was the last bit of quietness Matthew would know. He could not imagine the horror to come as Lee and Grant would race their armies south toward Richmond while engaging in almost continuous bloody combat.

The peacefully flowing Rapidan River separated the two armies that would soon be at war with each other again. North of the river, Grant, Meade, and the Army of the Potomac were making final preparations for offensive action while, south of the divide, Lee and his Army of Northern Virginia watched and waited for the enemy to make the first move. On May 4th, the Union army departed their winter camps in Culpeper County, crossed the river, and entered the densely tangled area known as the Wilderness. By noon, the Confederate soldiers were marching eastward to intersect with Grant's army. Matthew and the men of the 48th North Carolina traveled with General A. P. Hill's Third Corps on Orange Plank Road. The First Corps led by General James Longstreet was traveling northeast from Gordonsville and General Richard S. Ewell's Second Corps traveled via the Orange Turnpike. The men of Lee's army were moving fast; the plan was to trap the enemy while in the confines of that leafy, green maze. The claustrophobic woods and uneven ground beneath the bushes favored Lee's smaller army.[2] After a grueling march of almost twenty miles, Matthew and the men of the Third Corps halted for the night and bivouacked under the stars.

On May 5th, before dawn, Hill's men were on the march again. Matthew was near the front of the Confederate column as part of Cooke's brigade in Heth's division. In preparation for battle, the four regiments of the brigade were ordered into the forest as they approached the intersection of Orange Plank Road with Germanna Brock Road.[3] Matthew and his comrades were met with heavy enemy resistance as a storm of bullets mangled the thick undergrowth and also many soldiers. The historian for the 46th North Carolina, J. M. Waddell, wrote, "A butchery pure and simple it was..."[4] For more than two hours the brigades of Cooke and Kirkland "held 25,000 Yankees in check" for which they received praise from General Lee.[5] Matthew and the men of Cooke's brigade were assigned to the rear that night

Chapter Seven

where they fell asleep in a straw field. The soldiers were worried; Longstreet and his First Corps were still enroute. All hoped and prayed for their soon arrival.

On the morning of May 6th, most of the lines in Hill's Third Corps were in shambles and there was no plan for how to proceed without Longstreet's reinforcements.[6] When the Union offensive resumed, the Third Corps crumpled and the beleaguered brigades began to retreat. Lee's army was about to be annihilated. It was at that moment that Longstreet appeared atop his horse, kicking up the dust along Orange Plank Road. His men were running to the action, exhausted after a long march, but motivated anew when they realized they were the last hope for Lee's Army of Northern Virginia. Surely, Matthew heard the glorious commotion; there was wild cheering from all the men. Even General Lee, so elated and hopeful, began to trot his horse, Traveller, into position to ride into battle with Longstreet's Texas Brigade. He turned back after repeated chants from the soldiers, "Go back, General Lee! Go back!"[7] Matthew and his comrades were relieved that Longstreet's men and General Richard H. Anderson's division would be taking over for them.[8] They would now be out of the hottest of the battle. The desperate fighting ensued and throughout the afternoon there were attacks and counterattacks throughout the Wilderness.

When night came, the fighting ceased but there was no time to rest. The men scurried around searching for their loved ones and neighbors among the living and the dead.[9] Matthew was able to locate the Albright brothers and rejoiced at finding them well. In a letter to his parents dated May 6, 1864, Henry Albright wrote in haste, "The fighting has been desperate...M. C. Yow is unhurt."[10] Orange Plank Road stayed congested through the night, transporting the wounded and prisoners west to Orange Court House in wagons and then on their way to hospitals and prisons via train cars. The darkness and the smoke of the fires burning in the woods hampered the rescue efforts. The carnage was overwhelming. The grim task of burying the dead began but was never finished.

Grant decided on the morning of May 7th that he would move on from the Wilderness and by night both armies were marching away from that place of sheer terror. A place where, according to Grant's aide, Horace Porter, "It seemed as though Christian men had turned to fiends, and hell itself had usurped the place of earth."[11] As the men marched, they may have conversed about the changes in Lee's army. A. P. Hill, incapacitated due to the flare-up of a chronic illness, was temporarily replaced by General Jubal A. Early as the Third Corps commander. Longstreet, wounded by his own men, was replaced by Richard Anderson to command the First Corps. Stories were shared about the men of Ewell's Second Corps fighting on the turnpike near Saunders Field. The men marched south toward Richmond, on through the dark, hoping the worst lay behind them. But this was just the beginning of the Overland Campaign.

Lee's army won the race to Spotsylvania Court House. Throughout the night of May 8th, they built defensive earthworks between the Po and Ni Rivers that ran north of the town. The work was grueling and interrupted by episodes of fighting. One such episode occurred on May 10th when Matthew and his regiment were involved in a fight against General Francis C. Barlow's division of the Union Second Corps south of the Po River. The 48th North Carolina was severely shelled and the Federals set the woods on fire as they (the Federals) began to retreat.[12] Matthew and his comrades marched back to camp and may have heard the regimental bands of both armies volleying tunes back and forth. The story

Chapter Seven

goes that a Confederate band played "Nearer, My God, to Thee," and a Union band answered with "Dead March." The musical medley continued with patriotic songs and brought Yankee cheering and Rebel yells from the respective sides; then another tune rang out. The Confederate band played "Home Sweet Home," which brought wild cheering from both sides.[13] Oh, how Matthew and all the men of both armies missed their homes!

On the morning of May 12th, Union soldiers breached the fortifications at the tip of the Mule Shoe occupied by Ewell's Second Corps.[14] The attack began before dawn and lasted 22 hours amid a drenching rain. It was a savage struggle that was characterized by brutal hand-to-hand combat. Thousands of soldiers fought on what became known as the "Bloody Angle," a half square mile of red soil and mud. The 48th North Carolina was engaged, but the soldiers "...were not in the hottest of the battle."[15] They manned the works and covered for reinforcements who were sent into the fight.

The rain continued to pour for the next few days. Despite the inclement weather, Matthew and his comrades continued to construct better earthworks while dodging enemy artillery. Night attacks were anticipated, so the soldiers slept in the trenches with their weapons ready and their boots on. Life was miserable. Not only were the men deprived of sleep, but they also suffered due to an increase in pneumonia, dysentery, and seed tick wounds.[16] When the morning of May 17th came, the sun shone brightly and the mud began to dry. Perhaps Matthew and the others dreaded the beautiful spring weather because it was what Grant needed to initiate another attack. The Confederates watched and waited. At daybreak on May 18th, Grant's army assaulted the rebel fortifications one last time at Spotsylvania Court House, but the works were unassailable. Grant suspended the offensive and marched his army south. The race was on to a place even closer to the Confederate capital, the North Anna River.[17]

Matthew and the men of Hill's Third Corps left their earthworks on May 21st after dark.[18] They crossed the Po River and headed south, and by noon the next day had crossed the North Anna River. They proceeded east on the Virginia Central Railroad to Hewlett's Station and set up camp by evening. The next morning, May 23rd, Hill's men were ordered to Anderson's Tavern. This put them closer to Hanover Junction, a small railroad settlement, where Lee's army had begun to congregate.[19] There was enemy movement across the river, but Lee had determined that it was nothing to worry about. He told his corps commanders to allow their men to have a day of rest. The soldiers relaxed and many, Matthew most likely included, wrote letters home. May 23rd started out as a peaceful Monday. However, Lee had made a grave mistake. Grant's plan, devised the night before, was to attack the Confederates that very day. The battle would soon begin.

General Gouverneur Warren's Fifth Corps crossed the North Anna River at Jericho Mills during the late afternoon and aroused the Confederates from their complacency. Hill quickly deployed General Cadmus M. Wilcox's division into action before Warren had all of his men in line for battle. Even though the Confederates were unprepared and outnumbered, they were able to break the Union line and Warren's men scattered. The cannons began to boom more as Colonel Charles S. Wainwright's Union artillery increased their firing in response to the emergency. The noise was deafening and the Confederates were driven back, away from the river into the woods.

The men of Heth's division were deployed into action to support Wilcox. Matthew and the other men, while rushing west to enter the fray, were "exposed to an awful heavy shelling" from Wainwright's artillery which was "falling and bouncing thick on the ground."[20] Captain Lawhon[21] wrote that he remembered two casualties in Company D that day – his brother, Sergeant Cornelius Lawhon,[22] and Corporal Matthew C. Yow,[23] both killed with the same shot.[24] Walkup indirectly referred to Matthew in a diary entry of that day that read, "In endeavoring to advance back to North Anna, we got two men killed..."[25] According to information passed down to Catharine, Matthew died in Petersburg shortly after the incident. We know that a memorial meeting was held on Saturday, June 11, 1864, at Mount Olivet Lodge, No. 195,[26] which confirms he had died by then.[27]

Catharine received a letter from Captain Lawhon revealing the gruesome details about Matthew's wound. We have this information because when Catharine applied for a widow's pension in 1885, she transcribed the letter onto the application. Here is what she wrote.

∼

Hanover Junction, Va. May 25, 1864

Mrs. Nancy C. Yow:

Madam, it is my sad duty to communicate to you the death of your husband, Matthew C. Yow. He fell mortally wounded day before yesterday, October 5th,[28] while we were advancing on the Yankees, they shelling us severely. A solid shot cut his leg nearly off near the hip joint.

        Wm. H. Lawhon, Capt. Co. D 48th Reg't N. C. T.

Catharine and many people during that time were becoming more acquainted with death as the war raged on. The loss of so many men, some young and others in the prime of life, was unprecedented in American history. Many people in the county were mourning the loss of husbands, sons, fathers, and brothers. Now Catharine shared with them the most devastating of war's experiences. Death had come to her home.[29]

Catharine missed her husband but there was more to her loss than that. Before the war came, there were expectations about how life would end. Now, during the war, those Victorian customs based on the *ars moriendi* (the art of dying) to achieve the Good Death, were violated.[30] Many soldiers were deprived of the elements of the Good Death, two of which were dying at home surrounded by family and speaking the last words to give comfort and direction to the bereaved. Matthew, always aware of his mortality, had tried to prepare Catharine for his death. In his letters, he told her not to grieve so much about him and to raise the children to love the Lord. He often reassured her that if he died in battle, they would meet again in heaven where they would part no more. Matthew's written words were meant to console and support Catharine as if she and the children were at his side when he died.

But what about Matthew's consolation? Perhaps a comrade or a chaplain gave comfort to him in his final moments. If he remained conscious, he probably clutched his Bible or a letter from Catharine to his heart. This is how many Civil War soldiers died far from home and family.

Catharine had the sad duty to acquaint her children with the war's grimmest consequence – the death of their beloved Papa. The "little children," as Matthew referred to them in letters, had prayed for his safe return and now were told he would never come home. The children cherished the memories they had of Papa, such as sitting in his lap and eating peaches together. They treasured the gifts he gave to them and the sweet letters he wrote to them. Catharine and the children were thankful for the likeness he had sent to them almost two years earlier. The children would never forget their papa.

It is not known where Matthew was buried. His body was not returned or retrieved after his passing. In the midst of the Overland Campaign, homes and hospitals were full of wounded men who required the attention of those who were alive. Burying the dead was a task that could not be done with the same respect and dignity as earlier in the war. Many men were never buried. Some were buried in shallow graves where their remains were subjected to the elements and animal predators. Perhaps Matthew was buried in a mass grave at the Blandford Church Cemetery in Petersburg. There in a designated area are buried thirty thousand of the Confederate Dead.[31] Matthew's resting place is known only to God from where his body awaits the Day of Resurrection. His Christian faith rested on the hope that God, who would remember him, would reunite him in heaven one day with those he loved on Earth.

Matthew was mortally wounded on the first day of the battle at the North Anna River. His comrades missed him but time did not stand still; the battle went on. The next day the men of the 48th were stationed between the Little River and the Virginia Central Railroad as part of the western leg of Lee's clever design known as the inverted V.[32] As Union troops advanced on the morning of May 24th, the wedge did as Lee had hoped; it divided the enemy troops, thus making it difficult for them to attack. As fate would have it, Lee was unable to exercise the offensive option due to severe illness and his hesitancy to delegate leadership to a corps commander. Lee, confined to his tent, with a fever, called out through the hours, "We must strike them a blow!"[33] Because there was no one to take his place on the battlefield to direct the movement of troops, the opportunity passed; no advantage was gained from the ingenious formation.

Once again, the armies of Grant and Lee came to stalemate and by May 27th were traveling south again.

By the first day of June, both armies were concentrated at a place known as Cold Harbor. The men of the regiment fortified as well as they could with very few tools, all the while engaged in sporadic skirmishing. Colonel Walkup was sure that the troops would be well protected against any assault the enemy would send[34] and on June 3rd Cooke's brigade successfully repulsed the Union's attacks. According to Lawhon, "At no time during the war did the forty-eighth and twenty-seventh do better fighting."[35] The battle was a lopsided Confederate victory with the Union dead and wounded strewn in front of the Confederate works up and down the six-mile line.[36] The two armies spent the next nine days in the trenches baking in the sun and plagued by the suffocating dust. On the morning of June 13th, Grant and his army slipped away without notice while the regimental bands played. The Overland Campaign had come to an end.[37]

The Union troops crossed the James River and headed for Petersburg, Virginia. Grant's plan was to capture the strategic city with its many railroad connections in order to cut Richmond off from the rest of the Confederacy. General P. G. T. Beauregard's Confederate troops ably defended the city until most of Lee's army, including the 48th North Carolina, arrived by the 18th of June. Grant then turned his attention to the railroad system and devised ways to cripple service from the south. This was the beginning of a nine month siege.

On July 28th, the regiment, as part of Heth's division, was ordered to march north to where it was thought the Confederate capital was threatened. Two days later, after crossing the Appomattox River and heading for Richmond, the men heard a large explosion behind them. The troops returned to the trenches of Petersburg and took up positions in the very place where the

Chapter Seven

"blow-up" as they called it, occurred.[38] This is known as the Battle of the Crater which occurred on July 30, 1864.[39]

The following months brought even lower morale for the soldiers of Lee's army. The men of the 48th regiment were involved in the fighting near Globe Tavern and Reams Station in August which resulted in more disruption to the supply lines into Petersburg. The soldiers were dying from disease and battle wounds. Many were captured and some gave themselves up. In November, the Rebels were discouraged to hear that President Lincoln had won reelection. There was now no hope for a peace treaty with the North. The 48th North Carolina went into winter quarters at Hatcher's Run in late fall and experienced some picket skirmishes through the end of the year. During the early months of 1865 there was relative calm except for the ever present sniper and artillery attacks. February brought a surprise attack by Grant's soldiers at Hatcher's Run which lasted two days and weakened the Confederates supply-wagon traffic on the Boydton Plank Road.

The men were wearier than ever and began deserting at an alarming rate about which Colonel Walkup wrote often in his diary. On March 4, 1865, he recorded, "We have been decimated and more than decimated by desertion."[40] Not only did the men feel defeat was inevitable, they wanted to go home and protect their families from General Sherman's army.

Lee took the initiative one last time on March 25, 1865 at Fort Stedman. Cooke's brigade was put in reserve; the troops that made the assault were slaughtered, and the Confederate loss was great.[41] A week later, Union forces under General Sheridan attacked the Rebels at Five Forks. This was a significant win for Grant whose army now had access to the South Side Railroad. Colonel Walkup wrote to his wife that night and told her not to send anything to him. He explained, "We will be either killed or captured or the road will be destroyed before this letter reaches you."⁴² Grant attacked again on April 2nd, and the Confederate lines were broken. General A. P. Hill was killed in action that day. The next seven days were chaotic as the scattered men began the "memorable retreat to Appomattox Court House" where on Sunday, April 9, 1865, General Lee surrendered his Army of Northern Virginia to General Grant.⁴³ The 48th North Carolina, having had 1,300 men over the previous three years since its organization at Camp Mangum, had only about 100 members present on April 12th when the army was paroled.⁴⁴ Only two men from Company D were there.⁴⁵

The weary, hungry, and tattered Tar Heel soldiers began to find their way back home from the places of surrender. Others came out of hiding and others from places of captivity. Some were happy the war was over; they were ready to work hard and build back what they had lost during the war. Others were angry that Southern independence was not achieved; they held on to their animosity and participated in guerrilla warfare and horrific deeds after the war.

North Carolina, the state that hesitated to leave the Union and entered the Confederacy next to last, gave more men to the cause and sustained more losses than any of the other seceded states. There were 133,905 men who left their Tar Heel homes to fight; 40,275 did not return.⁴⁶ For every one of those men, including Matthew C. Yow, the grief of wives, children, and other loved ones, was carried into the generations that followed.

Those who survived that terrible conflict including Catharine Yow and her five children, felt profound loss until the day they died. Catharine, it is said, carried her husband's last letter in her apron pocket through all the years she outlived him, and was buried with it. Perhaps that last letter gave her some cheer, in the sense of encouragement, to do all she could do to take care of herself and the children. Perhaps it reminded Catharine, as many of his letters did, not to overly grieve so she

Chapter Seven

could focus on the future. Surviving was about finding reasons to keep living; surviving was also about finding ways to keep the memory alive of those who had died. Catharine, and all the survivors of that time, North and South, civilians and soldiers, free and newly emancipated, would forever remember their lost loved ones.

At Blandford Cemetery in Petersburg, Virginia is located a mass grave that contains the remains of 30,000 soldiers who died during the siege of 1864-65. Memorial Hill is divided into separate areas for the different Confederate states. The names of only 3,700 soldiers are known. Matthew's body may be among the unknown remains (image courtesy of Nancy Y. Holt).

This monument is located at North Anna Battlefield Park in Hanover County, Virginia. The descendants of Cpl. Michael Shortell of the 7th Wisconsin, erected it in his honor and in honor of "all the valiant men who lost their lives on the battlefields of North Anna." Shortell was killed at Jericho Mills on May 23, 1864. Inscribed on the monument is the last stanza of the poem "The Blue and the Gray" by Francis Miles Finch (image courtesy of Nancy Y. Holt).

Appendix A
Remembrance and Reconciliation

A few years ago, my husband, Steve, and I visited the North Anna Battlefield Park in Hanover County, Virginia. I wanted to better understand the place where my great-grandfather, Matthew C. Yow, had been mortally wounded on May 23, 1864. It was a beautiful summer day. The sunlight dappled in the treetops above and seemed to beckon us on into the woods where we hoped to learn more about earthworks, Lee's inverted V formation, and my ancestor's part in a little known Civil War battle at Jericho Mills.

We walked up and down hills and read the interpretive markers along the way. In the stillness of that day, with just the sound of the breeze and the flow of the river, I thought about my great-grandfather's struggles during the war and how much I wanted to better understand his story, as told through his letters. After a few hours, we exited the woods and approached the small and unassuming North Anna monument. I began to read the plaque and tears filled my eyes; it was in honor of a soldier whose name I knew not and inscribed on the monument was a poem I had never read. What a wonderful tribute of remembrance and reconciliation, I thought. I was inspired to learn more.

Michael Shortell, the soldier named on the monument, and "kept in eternal remembrance by his family," lived in the town of Stockton, Wisconsin in Portage County when the war began.[1] His parents, Michael and Joanna Shortell, were born in Ireland, and had immigrated to New Brunswick, Canada. They moved to Wisconsin in about 1850 when Michael was 10 years old. Michael enlisted into the Union Army on August 12, 1861, when he was twenty years old as a private in Company G of the 7th Wisconsin Infantry. According to the Roster of Wisconsin Volunteers,[2] he was wounded on September 14, 1862, at South Mountain, Maryland. He was captured at Gettysburg on July 1, 1863, and later released. By the time the 23-year-old soldier reached the North Anna River, he knew a good bit about the trials of battle. His regiment was part of the famed Iron Brigade[3] led by Colonel William W. Robinson, in the fourth division of General Gouverneur Warren's Fifth Corps.

Michael was killed in the line of battle shortly after Warren's Fifth Corps crossed the North Anna River and encountered Wilcox's division of A. P. Hill's Third Corps at Jericho Mills on the afternoon of May 23, 1864. Michael's parents were distraught to learn of their son's death and the seven younger children would forever miss their big brother. The descendants of two of Michael's sisters, Mary and Lucy, wanted to keep his memory alive so the monument was erected in his honor, but not only in his honor. It was erected in honor of the 4,200 men, including Matthew C. Yow, who died or were mortally wounded at the North Anna River between May 23rd and 26th, 1864.[4] The plaque refers to all of them, Confederate and Union, as valiant men. This was a conciliatory act on the part of the family.

The poem on the plaque I learned is the last stanza of "The

Appendix A

Blue and the Gray," written by Francis Miles Finch (1827-1907), an Ithaca, New York judge. Finch was inspired to write the poem when he read about a deed of remembrance performed by some women in Columbus, Mississippi in 1866. The story goes that the women went to the local cemetery where fallen Confederates were buried; they decorated their graves and also the ones of the few Union soldiers who were buried there. Their conciliatory deed also included sending notes of condolences to the families of the Union soldiers. Finch's poem, written as a tribute to the women, appeared for the first time in *The Atlantic Monthly* in 1867.[5] Based on this event, Columbus, Mississippi considers itself to be the first place to observe Memorial Day. Of course, that is a debate for another day as several American cities have made that claim.

Now when I visit the North Anna Battlefield Park, I think of two soldiers who fought during the Jericho Mills Battle: Corporal Matthew C. Yow and Corporal Michael Shortell, both valiant men who are worthy of remembrance.

The 48th North Carolina Infantry Regiment was organized at Camp Mangum near Raleigh on April 9, 1862. The regimental flag was issued to the unit's commander, Colonel Robert C. Hill, on April 29th. The many battles the regiment participated in are indicated by the white strips (applied post-war) sewn in angled rows. Some of the battles indicated on the remaining white strips are French's Farm, Harper's Ferry, Sharpsburg, Fredericksburg, Bristowe, Mine Run, Wilderness, Poe River, Spotsylvania, Cold Harbor, Reams Station, and Hatcher's Run. The flag was surrendered in April 1865 when the troops were paroled at Appomattox Court House, Virginia. The flag found its home with various individuals before being taken back to Raleigh in 1915 where it is now archived at the North Carolina Museum (photo courtesy of North Carolina Museum of History).

Appendix B
The Soldiers of Co. D of the 48th North Carolina Infantry

The names of the 149 men of Company D are listed on the following pages. These are the men with whom Matthew camped, marched, and fought during his time in the army. These soldiers did not have adequate clothing or shelter and were often hungry. Together, they fought not just the Yankees but an army of irritating insects such as flies and gnats. Many lost the fight against mosquitos and a host of invisible creatures that brought disease and death. These cousins, extended family members, neighbors, and strangers, became Matthew's comrades.

The following list allows us to see both personal and military information about each man at a glance. In parentheses next to each name is recorded the soldier's enlistment date, age, and occupation. What follows informs us about wounds, death, capture, and history of desertion. We can also figure out the collective story of the company concerning the number of casualties the men of the unit sustained. The information is found in Weymouth T. Jordan's book *North Carolina Troops, 1861-1865: A Roster* Vol. XI, pages 409-420.[1] The information is reliable because it is backed up by company rolls and other sources. There are segments of time for which company rolls are not available.[2] Therefore, we can be sure that casualties and desertions did occur (if listed), but not sure if they did or did not occur (if not listed). For example, a man who was wounded in 1865, from which time no company rolls survived and other records were not found, would not be counted as a casualty. We would not know that he had been wounded. We can say with confidence that in each category (wounds, died of wounds, died of disease, POW, and desertion), the number could be higher than what is shown here.

Of the 149 men of the company, the ages of 133 of them are recorded. The ages ranged from 17 to 66 years old. The median age was 26, meaning that half of the men in the company were between 17 and 26 and the other half were between 26 and 66. The average age was 27 years old.

Occupations were listed for 82 of the soldiers: farmers totaled 67, mechanics 10, and there were 2 laborers. There was one student, one tailor, and a merchant among the men of the company whose occupations were known.

Fifty-two men of Company D died during the war, which calculates to be 35 percent of the unit. The men died of combat injuries and, at an even greater rate, of disease. Fifteen men (10 percent) of the 48th North Carolina Co. D died of wounds and 37 men (25 percent) died of disease. The diseases listed most frequently that the soldiers succumbed to were diarrhea, typhoid fever, and pneumonia. Forty-six men (31 percent) were wounded during combat. From this data, we see that for every ten soldiers wounded, three died as a result.

Of the 149 men on the roster, there were 47 (31.5 percent) listed as prisoners of war. Two of the men were captured twice. Seven men were captured during the Battle of Sharpsburg in September of 1862. Ten men were captured during the Battle of

Appendix B

Bristoe Station in October of 1863. Five men were captured during the Overland Campaign and early months of the Petersburg siege in 1864 from Wilderness, Spotsylvania Court House, Cold Harbor, Hanover Junction, and Reams Station. Most of the men from this unit, however, were captured during the desperate last days of Lee's army in the spring of 1865. Seven men are recorded as having deserted to the enemy. The remaining 19 POWs were captured from Hatcher's Run, a hospital in Richmond, Fort Stedman, or somewhere near Petersburg. It is interesting to note that of the 47 POWs, only three died while in captivity: one of wounds incurred at the time of capture and two of disease. Most of the men were confined at Point Lookout in Maryland; the others spent time in the Old Capitol Prison in Washington, D.C., Newport News, Virginia, Forts Delaware and McHenry in Delaware, or Elmira, New York. After a while they were paroled, exchanged, joined the U.S. Army, or were released after taking the Oath of Allegiance.

The number of soldiers who suffered at least one casualty while in the unit was 103.[3] This means that 69 percent of the men in Company D, approximately, seven out of every ten, were either wounded, captured, or died during the war.

Fifty-nine men of the company (40 percent) chose to desert at some point during the war. Some men, such as Matthew, deserted with plans to return quickly and others never returned unless they were captured and forced to as a result. Some men went home to help and protect their families, some hid out or caused mischief, and others ran to the enemy and became captives. The desertion rate was very high toward the end of the war; the men were weary and there was little hope of a Southern victory.

In the group of about 100 soldiers of the 48th North Carolina Infantry, there were only two from Company D who made it to the village of Appomattox Court House on the day of surrender: Private Alexander Campbell and Captain W. H. H. Lawhon. In 1901, Lawhon wrote a regimental history praising the men of the 48th North Carolina "...as brave and as obedient as any soldiers in the Confederate army."4

Company D Soldiers

An asterisk indicates the soldier died during the war. A @ indicates the soldier had a history of desertion. There is more information about the soldiers in Jordan's roster, but this listing emphasizes personal and casualty information. There is an occasional fact given such as enlisting as a substitute or joining the U.S. Army.

Sgt. Joseph P. **Allen*** (3/13/62, 19, farmer) was wounded at or near Petersburg on 9/9/64 and died of wounds on 9/14/64.

Pvt. Raleigh S. **Allen** (3/13/62, 32, merchant)

Pvt. William H. **Baker** (2/25/62, 46, farmer) was captured at Bristoe Station 10/14/63, POW Point Lookout, MD.

Pvt. William **Ballard** (2/25/62, 28, farmer/mechanic) was wounded May 1864, captured at Hanover Junction 5/22/64, POW Point Lookout, MD. Joined the U.S. Army after taking the Oath of Allegiance. @

Pvt. Charles A. **Barnhart*** (8/8/62, 31) was wounded at Sharpsburg on 9/17/62, died of disease (chronic diarrhea) on 1/15/64.

Appendix B

Pvt. Stephen M. **Barr** (after 10/31/64) was captured at Hatcher's Run 3/31/65, POW Point Lookout, MD.

Pvt. Daniel **Beck*** (8/8/62, 35) died of disease (typhoid fever) on 11/22/62.

Pvt. George D. **Beck** (8/8/62, 33) @

Pvt. Malcolm **Black*** (2/25/62, 66, tailor) died of disease on 11/1/62.

Pvt. Malcolm A. **Black** (2/25/62, 30, farmer)

Pvt. Isaac **Brady*** (3/8/62, 45, farmer) was wounded at King's School House on 6/25/62 and died of wounds on 6/25/62.

Pvt. Wesley W. **Brady** (3/8/62, 17, farmer) was captured at or near Cold Harbor 6/4/64, POW Point Lookout, MD. Joined the U.S. Army after taking the Oath of Allegiance. @

Pvt. Horace A. **Bridges** (2/25/62, 25, farmer) was captured at Bristoe Station 10/14/63, POW Point Lookout, MD, again captured at or near Fort Stedman 3/25/65, POW Point Lookout, MD. @

Pvt. Joseph **Britt** (3/13/62, 23) was arrested for desertion and on or about 5/2/64 was court-martialed. @

Sgt. Andrew A. **Broadway** (8/8/62, 30) was captured at Ream's Station 8/25/64, POW Point Lookout, MD.

Cpl. Samuel W. **Broadway*** (8/8/62, 35) was wounded

(unknown battle) and died of disease (chronic diarrhea) on 10/8/64.

Pvt. Kelly **Bryant** (8/8/62, 24) was wounded at Fredericksburg on or about 12/13/62, captured at Hatcher's Run 4/2/65, POW Point Lookout, MD.

Pvt. Alexander **Campbell** (3/16/63, 25) surrendered at Appomattox Court House, VA on 4/9/65.

Sgt. George B. **Campbell*** (3/7/62, 22, farmer) was wounded at Sharpsburg on 9/17/62 and at Bristoe Station on 10/14/63, died of wounds on 10/25/63.

Pvt. Alex A. **Clouts** (after 10/31/64) was captured at Hatcher's Run 3/31/65, POW Point Lookout, MD.

Pvt. Zack **Coggin*** (8/8/62, 18) was wounded at Fredericksburg on 12/13/62 and died of wounds on 12/13/62.

Pvt. Hugh B. **Cox** (11/1/64) was wounded in December 1864.

Pvt. Solomon **Craven** (2/25/62, 41, mechanic) was wounded at Sharpsburg on 9/17/62.

Pvt. Amos **Crotts** (9/23/64) deserted to the enemy on or about 3/16/65, POW Washington, D. C. @

Pvt. Andrew C. **Crotts** (8/8/62, 24) was captured in hospital at Richmond 4/3/65, POW Newport News, VA. @

Appendix B

Pvt. George **Crotts** (8/8/62, 21) was captured at or near Sharpsburg, MD 9/17/62. @

Pvt. William **Crotts*** (8/8/62, 23) died of disease in October 1862.

Pvt. Baxter **Davis** (3/13/62, 22, farmer) was captured near Petersburg, VA 4/2/65, POW Point Lookout, MD. @

Pvt. Charles **Davis*** (4/28/62, 19) died of disease (typhoid fever) on 11/11/62.

Pvt. Enoch **Davis** (4/28/62, 26) @

Pvt. Henry **Davis** (8/8/62, 27) was wounded at Bristoe Station on 10/14/63, captured at or near Fort Stedman on 3/25/65, POW Point Lookout, MD.

Pvt. Raleigh **Davis** (3/13/62, 25, farmer) was wounded at Fredericksburg on 12/13/62 and at Bristoe Station on 10/14/63, captured at or near Hatcher's Run 3/25/65, POW Point Lookout, MD.

Pvt. Burwell **Deaton*** (3/13/62, 25, farmer) was wounded at Sharpsburg on or about 9/17/62 and died of wounds on 10/31/62.

Pvt. John M. **Deaton** (3/13/62, 23, farmer) @

Pvt. Samuel J. **Dorsett*** (8/8/62, 19) died of disease (typhoid fever) on 11/25/62.

Pvt. William Wesley **Dorsett** (8/8/62, 21) was captured at Hatcher's Run 4/2/65, POW Point Lookout, MD.

Pvt. Henry **Evans** * (2/25/62, 30, farmer) died of disease on or about 5/12/62.

Pvt. Henry A. **Fields*** (3/7/62, 19, farmer) died of disease on 11/25/62.

Pvt. Joseph H. **Fields** (12/5/64) was wounded near Petersburg on 2/7/65, deserted to the enemy on or about 3/24/65, POW Washington, D. C. @

Pvt. Gabriel **Fine** (8/8/62, 37, farmer) enlisted as a substitute and was wounded at Fredericksburg on 12/13/62, wounded and captured at Wilderness 5/5/64, POW Elmira, New York.

Pvt. Jonathan S. **Fine** (8/8/62, 22) was captured at Hatcher's Run 4/2/65, POW Point Lookout, MD.

Pvt. James **Forrest** (8/8/62) was wounded at Fredericksburg on 12/13/62.

Pvt. Isaac **Freeman*** (3/13/62, 26, farmer) was wounded at Sharpsburg on 9/17/62, captured at Bristoe Station 10/14/63, POW Point Lookout, MD, died of disease (diarrhea) on 11/16/63 while in captivity.

Cpl. James A. **Freeman*** (5/14/62, 22) was captured at Bristoe Station on 10/14/63, POW at Point Lookout, MD, died of unknown cause (possibly disease) while on way home for furlough on 3/20/65 or 4/15/65.

Appendix B

Pvt. John W. **Freeman** (2/25/62, 18, farmer) @

Pvt. M. C. **Gallimore*** (8/8/62, 19) died of disease on 11/5/62.

Pvt. William **Gallimore*** (8/8/62, 19) died of disease on 10/5/62.

Pvt. William **Gilmore*** (2/25/62, 43, farmer) was wounded at or near King's School House on 6/25/62 and died of wounds on 6/25/62.

Pvt. G. W. **Green** (8/8/62, 30, farmer) was discharged on 8/31/62 due to chronic inflammation of the knee joint.

Pvt. Reuben **Hancock** (3/13/62, 21, farmer) was wounded at Fredericksburg on 12/13/62, deserted to the enemy on or about 3/24/65, POW at Washington, DC. @

Pvt. John M. **Harrington*** (2/25/62, 20, farmer) died of disease (pneumonia) on 6/27/62.

Pvt. Solomon S. **Hearn*** (8/8/62, 30) was wounded accidentally at or near Sharpsburg on 9/18/62 and in May 1864, died of disease (dysentery) on 1/30/65.

Pvt. Calvin **Hendley** (5/6/64) deserted to the enemy on 3/17/65, POW Washington D. C. @

Pvt. John **Hudson** (8/8/62, 46) enlisted as a substitute.

Pvt. James M. **Hunsucker** (2/26/62, 40, mechanic) was

wounded at Hatcher's Run on 2/5/65, deserted to the enemy on or about 3/24/65, POW Washington D. C. @

Pvt. Stephen **Huntley** (after 10/31/64) was captured near Petersburg 4/2/65, POW Point Lookout, MD.

Pvt. Samuel **Jackson*** (2/25/62, 37, farmer) died of disease (chronic diarrhea) on 12/3/62.

Pvt. Brantley Benjamin **Johnson** (3/8/62, 18, farmer) was wounded in 1863 (date not specified) at Wilderness, VA. @

Pvt. Duncan M. **Johnson*** (2/25/62, 46, mechanic) died of disease 8/2/62.

Pvt. John H. **Kessley*** (8/8/62, 26) was wounded at Sharpsburg on 9/17/62 and died of wounds on 9/17/62.

Pvt. Rials **Key** (2/25/62, 39, mechanic) was captured at Bristoe Station 10/14/63, POW at Old Capitol Prison in Washington D. C.

Pvt. James H. **Lambeth** (8/8/62, 23) was captured at Hatcher's Run 4/2/65, POW Point Lookout, Md.

1st Sgt. Cornelius **Lawhon*** (5/14/62, 29) was wounded at the North Anna River near Hanover Junction on 5/23/64 and died of wounds on 5/23/64. He was killed with the same cannon ball that mortally wounded Cpl. Matthew C. Yow.

Neill **Leach** (unknown) served in this company according to NC pension records.

Appendix B

Pvt. James H. **Lewis** (2/25/62, 18, farmer) survived the war according to NC pension records.

Pvt. W. G. **Lewis** (3/10/62, 21) did not report for duty, listed as a deserter on 12/10/62. @

Pvt. Allen C. **McLean*** (2/28/62, 18, farmer) died of disease (pneumonia) on 11/14/62.

Pvt. Archibald **McLean** (5/28/63) previously served as private in Co. C. 35th NC Regiment and was transferred to this company in exchange for Pvt. Daniel R. McRae, captured at Bristoe Station 10/14/63, POW at Old Capitol Prison in Washington, D. C.

Pvt. Hector **McNeill*** (2/27/62, 33, farmer) died of disease (pneumonia and/or typhoid fever) on 12/7/62. @

Pvt. Noah **McNeill** * (2/27/62, 21, farmer) died of disease on 5/4/63.

Pvt. M. J. **McPhail*** (2/27/62, 22, farmer) was wounded at Sharpsburg on 9/17/62 and died of wounds on 11/15/62.

Pvt. Daniel R. **McRae** (3/7/62, 22, farmer) was transferred to Co. C. 35th NC Regiment on or about 5/28/63, in exchange for Pvt. Archibald McLean.

Pvt. George W. **Maddox** (3/3/62, 21, farmer) survived the war according to NC pension records.

Cpl. Benjamin **Malone** (2/25/62, 35, farmer) was captured at Hatcher's Run 3/31/65, POW Point Lookout, MD. @

Pvt. Peter J. **Mangum** (Jul-Sept 1863) was captured from hospital in Richmond on 4/3/65, POW at Newport News, VA.

Pvt. Malphus **Mathis*** (2/27/62, 22, mechanic) died of disease (pneumonia) in December 1862. @

Pvt. Joseph J. **May** (8/8/62, 19)

Sgt. Thomas A. **May** (8/8/62, 30, farmer) was captured at or near Sharpsburg on or about 9/17/62, POW Fort McHenry, MD., exchanged 11/10/62, captured at Hatcher's Run 4/2/65, POW Point Lookout, MD.

Pvt. George W. **Melton** (3/13/62, 18, farmer) deserted on 9/21/62. @

Pvt. B. F. **Miller*** (8/8/62, 25) died of disease on 10/31/62.

Pvt. J. W. E. **Moore** (3/13/62, 34, farmer) deserted on 8/8/62. @

Pvt. Edward D. **Morgan** (3/13/62, 19, farmer) was captured at Bristoe Station 10/14/63, POW Old Capitol Prison in Washington, D. C. @

Pvt. James G. **Morgan** (3/13/62, 43, farmer) was wounded at Sharpsburg on or about 9/17/62.

Appendix B

Pvt. Nathaniel **Morgan** (3/13/62, 28, farmer) deserted on 12/10/62. @

Pvt. Daniel **Morris*** (2/25/62, 28, mechanic) died of disease in May 1862.

Pvt. Jefferson C. **Myers** (8/8/62, 21, farmer) was wounded at Sharpsburg on 9/17/62. @

Pvt. Jesse B. **Parish*** (3/13/62, 20, laborer) was left sick near Winchester, Virginia, in October 1862, and died on an unknown date. Place and cause of death not reported.

Pvt. Thomas **Parish*** (3/7/62, 27, farmer) was captured in hospital at Richmond on 4/3/65, POW Newport News, VA, died of disease (acute diarrhea) on 5/29/65.

Pvt. David C. **Paschal** (2/25/62, 20, mechanic) was wounded at Fredericksburg on 12/13/62. @

Pvt. Nathan **Paschal*** (2/25/62, 33, mechanic) died at home of disease on 7/23/63.

Sgt. Baxter C. **Phillips** (2/25/62, 20, farmer) was wounded at Fredericksburg on 12/13/62. @

Ed **Phillips** (unknown) served in this company according to NC pension records.

Pvt. Eli **Phillips*** (2/25/62, 23, farmer) died of disease (typhoid fever) on or about 8/6/62.

Pvt. Martin C. **Phillips** (2/25/62, 26, student) was wounded at Fredericksburg on 12/13/62, captured at Bristoe Station on 10/14/63, POW Point Lookout, MD. @

Pvt. Stephen **Phillips*** (2/25/62, 52, farmer) died of disease (pneumonia) on or about 12/26/62.

Pvt. William L. **Phillips** (3/13/62, 22) was twice transferred to Castle Thunder Prison, Richmond, in 1864 from a hospital in Richmond for unknown reasons. @

Pvt. William **Pool*** (2/25/62, 22, farmer) died of disease (enteritis) on or about 6/1/64. @

Pvt. Robert **Rice** (8/8/62, 40) enlisted as a substitute and deserted five days later. @

Pvt. E. **Rich** (later than 10/31/64) deserted to the enemy on or about 3/24/65, POW Washington D. C. @

Pvt. David **Richardson** (3/13/62, 21, farmer) @

Pvt. Enoch **Richardson** (3/13/62, 35, farmer) deserted on 8/8/62. @

Pvt. John C. **Richardson** (3/13/62, 24, farmer) @

Cpl. James **Riddle*** (3/10/62, 52, mechanic) died of disease on 5/3/62.

Pvt. Henry **Roberson** (8/8/62, 35) @

Appendix B

Pvt. Abner **Rodgers** (2/25/62, 17, laborer)

Pvt. Enoch **Rouse** (3/13/62, 29, farmer) deserted on 12/10/62. @

Pvt. Simon **Sanders** (3/13/62, 26, farmer) was wounded and captured at Sharpsburg on 9/17/62, POW Fort Delaware, DE, wounded at Wilderness on 5/5/64. @

James **Seagroves** (unknown) served in this company according to NC pension records.

Pvt. Burwell H. **Short*** (2/25/62, 39) was wounded at or near King's School House on 6/25/62, died of wounds on 6/25/62.

Pvt. Daniel F. **Sinclair** (3/13/62, 30, farmer) was wounded at Cold Harbor on 6/3/64.

Sgt. Daniel M. **Sinclair** 2/25/62, 18) @

Pvt. Elias **Smith*** (2/25/62, 36, farmer) died of disease (pneumonia) on 11/25/62.

Pvt. Thomas **Smith** (8/8/62, 30) was wounded at Sharpsburg on 9/17/62, wounded again at Wilderness on or about 5/5/64. @

Pvt. Henry A. **Spence** (8/8/62, 29) was captured at Bristoe Station on 10/14/63, POW Point Lookout, MD.

Pvt. William A. **Stedman** (2/25/62, 26, farmer) was captured at or near Fort Stedman on 3/25/65, POW Point Lookout, MD.

Pvt. Enoch **Stewart** (2/27/62, 23, farmer) was discharged for unknown reason on 5/23/62.

Pvt. Robert B. **Stewart** (2/27/62, 27, farmer) was wounded at Bristoe Station in October 1863. @

1st Sgt. Samuel D. **Stewart*** (5/14/62, 32) was wounded and captured at Sharpsburg on 9/17/62, POW, paroled on or about 9/27/62, wounded again between January to April, 1863, died of wounds on or about 5/1/63.

Pvt. Andrew J. **Stutts** (3/13/62, 33, farmer) was wounded at King's School House on 6/25/62.

Pvt. Cornelius A. **Stutts** (4/28/62, 23) was captured near Petersburg on 4/2/65, POW Point Lookout, MD. @

Pvt. G. L. M. **Stutts** (3/10/64) was last reported in the records of the company on 6/25/64.

Pvt. George D. **Stutts** (2/27/62, 20, farmer) deserted on 8/27/62. @

Pvt. Henry W. **Stutts** (3/7/62, 32, farmer) was wounded at Sharpsburg on 9/17/62, captured at Hatcher's Run on 4/1/65, POW Point Lookout, MD.

Pvt. John H. **Stutts** (3/12/62, 55, farmer) was wounded at Fredericksburg on 12/13/62. @

Pvt. William C. **Stutts** (2/26/62, 44, farmer) deserted to the enemy on or about 3/16/65, POW Washington, D. C. @

Appendix B

Pvt. Franklin **Sullivan*** (8/8/62, 19) was wounded at Sharpsburg on 9/17/62, died of wounds on 9/17/62.

Pvt. Isaac McLendon **Sullivan** (4/29/62, 23) was listed as a deserter on or about 5/1/64. @

Pvt. Henry F. **Swicegood** (8/8/62, 35, farmer) deserted on 9/7/62 and was discharged on 11/14/62 by reason of tuberculosis ("phthisis"). @

Pvt. C. T. **Taylor*** (8/8/62, 23) was wounded at Sharpsburg on 9/17/62, died of wounds and/or chronic diarrhea on 12/8/62.

Pvt. D. W. **Taylor*** (8/8/62, 25) was wounded and captured at Sharpsburg on 9/17/62, paroled on or about 9/29/62, died of wounds on 11/30/62.

Pvt. W. B. **Teague** (8/8/62, 19) deserted on 9/2/62. @

Pvt. E. F. **Wadford*** (8/8/62, 20) was captured at Sharpsburg on 9/17/62, POW Fort Delaware, DE, died prior to 2/26/64, reason unknown.

Pvt. Calvin **Wallace** (9/28/64)

Pvt. Eli **Wallace** (2/25/62, 17, farmer) was wounded at Sharpsburg on 9/17/62.

Pvt. John M. **Wallace** (2/28/62, 17, farmer) was wounded at Fredericksburg on 12/13/62, captured at Spotsylvania Court House on 5/12/64, POW Point Lookout, MD, released after taking the Oath of Allegiance and joining the U.S. Army.

Pvt. W. S. **Ward*** (8/8/62, 28) died of disease (pneumonia) on 11/24/62.

Pvt. W. W. **Ward** (8/8/62, 26) was listed as a deserter and dropped from the rolls of the company on or about 5/1/64. @

Pvt. Alexander **West*** (8/8/62, 26) died of disease (chronic diarrhea) on 5/27/64. @

Pvt. George W. **Williams** (2/28/62, 18) was listed as a deserter and dropped from the rolls of the company on or about 5/1/64. @

Pvt. Harbert **Williams** (2/26/62, 22, farmer) was wounded at Sharpsburg on 9/17/62, listed as a deserter and dropped from the rolls of the company on or about 5/1/64. @

Pvt. John P. **Williams** (8/8/62, 30) @

Pvt. Jonathan J. **Williams** (8/8/62, 32) was captured in hospital at Richmond on 4/3/65, POW Newport News, VA. @

Pvt. James **Wood** (2/25/62, 33, farmer)

Pvt. Levi **Wright** (3/13/62, 46, mechanic) was captured at Bristoe Station on 10/14/63, POW Point Lookout, MD. @

Pvt. H. S. **Young*** (8/8/62, 27) died of disease ("erysipelas" a bacterial skin infection) on 11/29/63. @

Pvt. Andrew C. **Yow*** (3/10/62, 28, farmer) died of disease (chronic rheumatism) on 2/12/63. @

Appendix B

Pvt. David D. **Yow** (3/10/62, 26, farmer) was discharged on 5/23/63 for unknown reason. We know from Matthew's letters that the reason was due to health.

Cpl. Matthew C. **Yow*** (2/28/62, 34, farmer) was wounded at the North Anna River near Hanover Junction on or about 5/23/64 and died of wounds in June 1864. @

Pvt. William **Yow*** (3/10/62, 24, farmer) died of meningitis on July 7, 1862.

The Shiloh Church Cemetery is in Randolph County, North Carolina. Many in the Albright and Yow families are buried there (image courtesy of Nancy Y. Holt).

Appendix C
Yow and Albright Family Trees

The following ancestral trees help us to visualize the relationships of the people in the Yow and Albright families who lived during the time of the Civil War. These are some of the people with whom Matthew and Catharine corresponded about through their writing.

In addition to seeing how people are connected, these trees also help us to see the extent of the two families' involvement and loss during the war. At a glance, we can see how widespread death and suffering were. We see that of the eleven soldiers on these trees, five did not return. These odds of not returning from war, in this small sample size, are higher than what was seen throughout North Carolina which was 30 percent.[1]

A conservative estimate for the death rate for all Confederate soldiers is that one in five died during the conflict. Some historians argue that the estimate should be closer to one in four.[2]

I Hope You Will All Remember Me

The Yow Family Tree

Henry Yow (1806-1871) m. Nancy Elizabeth Jones
(1807-1851)
(Matthew C. Yow's parents and siblings)
Henry and Nancy had eleven children

<u>Matthew C. Yow</u> (1828-1864) m. Nancy Catharine Albright
(1830-1919)
Rebecca Yow (1830-unknown)
Elizabeth Yow (1832-unknown)
Julia A. Yow (1832-1910) m. *John Lewis Maness* (1824-1910)
Amelia Yow (c. 1834-1894) m. William N. Brower (1825-1905)
Sarah Yow (c. 1838-unknown)
Isaac Yow (c. 1838-1906) m. Dorcas S. Maness (1840-1906)
Simeon Jones Yow (1840-1900) m. Mary E. Harrison (1843-1931)
Mary E. Yow (1841-1917) m. <u>*Jesse Brown*</u> (1839-1863)[3]
William A. Yow (1845-1918) m. Martha J. Garner (1847-1940)
Lydia A. Yow (1848-1915) m. A. T. Harrison (1851-1897)

Civil War Soldier
<u>Soldier died during the Civil War</u>

Appendix C

The Albright Family Tree

Joseph Albright (1794-1876) m. Nancy Whitsitt (1799-1882)
(Catharine Albright Yow's parents and siblings)
Joseph and Nancy had eleven children

Jane Albright (1819-1852) m. Anthony T. Rich (1820-1894)
 John N. Rich (1844-1903) was one of their children.
Elizabeth Albright (1821-1851)
Mary Eleanor Albright (1824-1884) m. Thomas G. Craven
 (abt.1825-1893)
<u>William Stockard Albright</u> (1826-1864) m. Nancy E. Lawrence
 (1835-1901)
Joseph Gibbs Albright (1828-1848)
Nancy Catharine Albright (1830-1919) m. <u>Matthew C. Yow</u>
 (1828-1864)
Kizzie R. Albright (1832-1908)
Youthey Ann Albright (1834-1913) m. Joshua Brown
 (c. 1820-unknown)
Henry Alexander Albright (1836-1919) m. Margaret E. Farrell
 (1834-1909)
John Enslup Albright (1839-1910) m. Elizabeth A. Ward
 (1841-1896)
Rachel Delilah Albright (1841-1918) m. <u>Lawrence M. Ward</u>
 (1834-1864)[4]

Civil War Soldier
<u>Soldier died during the Civil War</u>

I Hope You Will All Remember Me

The Children of Matthew and Catharine Yow

William Henry Yow (1854-1934) m. Mariah E. Craven (1860-1914)
Nancy Elizabeth Yow (1856-1925)
Mary Jane Yow (1858-1929) m. James W. Hayes (1852-1933)
Joseph Gibbs Yow (1860-1929) m. Ada Jane Brown (1870-1932)
John Matthew Yow (1862-1936) m. Leola A. King (1888-1971)

Catharine moved closer to her parents and siblings in 1864 after Matthew died. She was a 34-year-old widow with five young children. She needed the extra support now that she knew her husband would not be returning from the war. Catharine and the five children made their home on a fifty-acre portion of land in Randolph County deeded to her by her father, Joseph Albright. According to the 1870 United States census, Catharine farmed and the children attended school.

The census of 1880 shows Catharine living at the same place with four of the children. Her daughter, Mary Jane, had left the home to be married by that time. She did not go far though; she lived on a portion of her mother's land and her husband farmed. During the decade Henry and Joseph found wives and left the home. They were both farmers, Henry in Randolph County and Joseph in Moore County. The 1900 United States census shows Catharine living at the farm with John and Nancy. John, 38 years old, was listed as head of the household with farming as his occupation. During the decade John was married and relocated near Seagrove, still in Randolph

Appendix C

County, where he became a merchant and pottery maker. His mother and sister went with him and were always a part of his family. Catharine died on September 20, 1919. She was almost 90 years old. She is buried at the Shiloh Church Cemetery in Ramseur, North Carolina.

Before Catharine's death she had become the grandmother of 29 children. The last grandchild, the father of this writer, was born two years after Catharine's death. There are many people in the counties of Moore and Randolph, throughout North Carolina, and outside of the state, that have descended from Matthew, Catharine, and their children. The family tree continues to grow.

Henry, Nancy, Jane, and John are buried at the Shiloh Church Cemetery in Randolph County where their mother is buried. Joseph is buried in Moore County at the Brown Family Cemetery. All is quiet at those places; there is no war or fighting. Matthew, Catharine, and the children are at peace now. We, who visit their grave sites, remember them with sorrow and love.

Notes

Introduction

1. *Semi-Weekly Observer*, Fayetteville, North Carolina, Nov. 18, 1851, 3. Death notice of "Elizabeth Yow," Matthew's mother. In the notice she is referred to as "a burning and shining light...a truly devoted Christian."
2. *Semi-Weekly Observer*, Fayetteville, North Carolina, Nov. 10, 1864, 2.
3. Manley Wade Wellman, *The Story of Moore County: Two Centuries of a North Carolina Region* (Southern Pines, N.C.: Moore County Historical Association, 1974), 55-65. Coal deposits in the northern part of Moore County brought prosperity to the area. The Deep River Mining and Transportation Company was formed in 1851 to meet the challenge. Business boomed in the pine forests where timber was felled for making barges to transport coal and for constructing the county's first plank road. There was also the production of turpentine and tar from the pine trees. By the end of the decade the Western Railroad, which ran from Fayetteville to the northeastern part of Moore County, was transporting coal. The economy was healthy and men worked in a variety of related occupations including wagon makers, mechanics, miners, and more. There were also improvements in the education and postal services. In the words of Wellman on page 65, "What could stop the happy, vigorous development of Moore County? War could stop it. And war was coming."
4. Michael C. Hardy, *North Carolina in the Civil War* (Charleston: The History Press, 2011), 10. The population of North Carolina in 1860 was 992,622 people and 331,059 of those were enslaved. The enslaved people were owned by slightly more than 27 percent of the population. There is no mention in Matthew's letters about people in his or Catharine's families who owned enslaved people. It appears that the couple did not participate in the institution although there is proof that their parents did. According to the slave schedules, Matthew's father owned three Black Americans in 1850 and Catharine's father owned one Black American in 1850 and in 1860. We do not know what Matthew's thoughts were about slavery since his letters do not mention the issue.
5. William Henry was known by his middle name Henry. Mary Jane's name was often shortened to Jane.
6. John G. Barrett, *The Civil War in North Carolina* (Chapel Hill: The University of North Carolina Press, 1963), 3.
7. Barrett, *The Civil War in North Carolina*, 4.

Notes

8. Wellman, *The Story of Moore County*, 67. Although the plan to have a convention to consider secession failed by a narrow margin in the state, the men of Moore County voted overwhelmingly against a convention: 1,257 to 135.
9. "Company D, 48th N.C. Assembles at Buffalo Church," *Weekly Observer*, Fayetteville, North Carolina, April 7, 1862, 3. M. C. Yow is not listed but there could have been a misprint. W. C. Yow is listed and there was not a Yow on the company's roster with those initials.
10. Weymouth Jordan, *North Carolina Troops, 1861-1865, A Roster*, University of North Carolina Press, 1987, v. XI, 409-420 (hereinafter "*Roster*").
11. W. H. H. Lawhon, "48th North Carolina Regimental History" in Walter Clark, ed., *History of the Several Regiments and Battalions from North Carolina*, Goldsboro, 1901, v. 3, 114 (hereinafter "Forty-Eighth Regiment").
12. Jordan, *Roster*, v. XI, 409-420. See information concerning the noncommissioned officers and privates of Company D of the 48th NC in Appendix B.
13. Robert Clinton Hill (1833-1863) – Colonel 48th NC previously served in the Artillery Corps (apparently as a recruiter and staff officer). Also served previously as assistant adjutant general (major) on the staff of General Robert A. Toombs and the staff of General Lawrence O'B. Branch. Appointed colonel of this regiment on April 9, 1862. Reported absent sick in May-June 1863. Died at home in Iredell County on December 4, 1863, of "neuralgia." Jordan, *Roster*, v. XI, 368.
14. Samuel Hoey Walkup (1818-1876) – Colonel 48th NC was elected lieutenant colonel on April 9, 1862, of the 48th NC Infantry. He was promoted to colonel on December 4, 1863. He was wounded at Fredericksburg, Virginia, December 13, 1862, and again at or near Wilderness, Virginia, in May of 1864. Surrendered at Appomattox Court House, Virginia, April 9, 1865. Jordan, *Roster*, v. XI, 369.
15. Benjamin Robinson Huske (1829-1862) – Major 48th NC previously served as captain of Company D of this regiment. Appointed major on April 9, 1862, and transferred to the Field and Staff. Wounded in the right foot at King's School House, Virginia, June 25, 1862. Died at or near Richmond, Virginia, July 15, 1862. Jordan, *Roster*, v. XI, 369, 408.
16. Hardy, *North Carolina in the Civil War*, 19.
17. The regiments that were part of Ransom's brigade in addition to the 48th NC at this time were the 24th NC, 25th NC, 26th NC, 35th NC, and 49th NC. Jordan, *Roster*, v. XI, 364.
18. Also known as the battle of King's School House, French's Field, or Oak Grove. This was the beginning of General Robert E. Lee's command of the Army of Northern Virginia. Lee had been appointed as the Confederate commander on June 1, 1862, at the conclusion of the Battle of Seven Pines (May 31-June 1) when General Joseph E. Johnston was wounded.

Notes

19. Kemp Burpeau, *Writings of a Rebel Colonel: The Civil War Diary and Letters of Samuel Walkup, 48th North Carolina Infantry* (Jefferson, N. C. : McFarland, 2021), 98.
20. The Battle of Second Manassas (or Second Bull Run) was fought August 28-30, 1862, and was a Confederate victory. This victory enabled the Army of Northern Virginia to cross the Potomac River and advance into Maryland, outside of Southern territory.
21. This is also known as the Battle of Sharpsburg.
22. Lawhon, "Forty-Eighth Regiment," 116.
23. Matthew C. Yow (1828-1864) – Corporal 48th NC was born in Moore County where he resided as a farmer prior to enlisting in Moore County at age 34, February 28, 1862. Mustered in as private. Deserted on September 7, 1862. Arrested and sent to camp on October 4, 1862. Reported present in January-June, 1863. Promoted to corporal in July 1863-April 1864. Reported present in March-April 1864. Wounded in the side at the North Anna River, Near Hanover Junction, Virginia, on or about May 23, 1864, by the same cannon ball that killed 1st Sergeant Cornelius Lawhon of this company. Died in hospital at Petersburg, Virginia, in June 1864, of wounds. Jordan, *Roster*, v. XI, 419.
24. Zebulon B. Vance was North Carolina's third war time governor. When Gov. Ellis died in July 1861, Henry Clark, the president of the Senate, replaced him. Vance was elected as governor in 1862.
25. S. H. Walkup Lt. Col. S. H. Walkup to Gov. Zebulon Vance, October 11, 1862, in the Governor's Papers, North Carolina State Archives, Raleigh, NC.
26. Lawhon, "Forty-Eighth Regiment," 117.
27. Jordan, *Roster*, v. XI, 365.
28. Matthew was very homesick at this time. This is confirmed in a letter written by Henry Albright to his parents dated May 16, 1863, in which he wrote, "I have just returned from the camps at Goldsboro. I saw Matthew Yow... Matthew is well, though I am sorry to say very much dissatisfied. He studies a great deal about his family. I hope his separation may not be long." From the unpublished letters of Henry A. Albright in the possession of Larry R. Yow.
29. Samuel H. Walkup, "Report of 48th Regiment N. C. T.," *The Daily Progress*, Raleigh, North Carolina, Feb. 24, 1864, 2.
30. Barrett, *The Civil War in North Carolina*, 182.
31. Reorganization occurred in the Army of Northern Virginia after the mortal wounding of General Stonewall Jackson at Chancellorsville in May 1863. Richard S. Ewell was promoted to second corps command and A. P. Hill to third corps command. The 48th NC remained in A. P. Hill's Third Corps for the remainder of the war.
32. Samuel H. Walkup, "Report of 48th Regiment N. C. T.," *The Daily Progress*, Raleigh, North Carolina, Feb. 24, 1864, 2. In this article Walkup

Notes

reported that eight men were killed, 116 wounded, and 50 taken as prisoners during the Battle of Bristoe Station.

Chapter One

1. Outliers were men who dodged the draft. Hardy, *North Carolina in the Civil War*, 45.
2. Bell Irvin Wiley, *The Life of Johnny Reb: The Common Soldier of the Confederacy* (1943; repr., Baton Rouge: Louisiana State University Press, 2008), 200.
3. Wiley, *The Life of Johnny Reb*, 199.
4. Wiley, *The Life of Johnny Reb*, 216.
5. This letter was sent to Matthew's father, Henry Yow (1806-1871), and his second wife, Elizabeth R. Maness Yow (1832-1908), and their family. Matthew's mother, Nancy Elizabeth Jones Yow (1807-1851), passed away before he and Catharine were married.
6. Camp Mangum was an army camp near Raleigh, North Carolina.
7. The Confederate Congress allowed a volunteer to provide a substitute.
8. Colonel Robert Clinton Hill was known for being strict. W. H. H. Lawhon wrote in his regimental history that he "...was a very fine military man, very strict and much beloved by his men." Lawhon, "Forty-Eighth Regiment," 123.
9. Henry Alexander Albright (1836-1919) – 2nd lieutenant Co. C 10th NC Light Artillery was born in Alamance County and was by occupation a deputy sheriff prior to enlistment in Randolph County at age 25, June 8, 1861 for the war. Mustered in as corporal and appointed sergeant August 20, 1861. Promoted to 1st sergeant July 26, 1862. Promoted to 2nd lieutenant May 6, 1863. Present or accounted for through February 1865. Paroled at Appomattox Court House, Va., April 9, 1865. Jordan, *Roster*, v. 1, 62. Henry was Catharine's brother. After the war, Henry married and raised five children in Randolph County. He was ordained as a minister at the age of 32. He is buried at Shiloh Baptist Church Cemetery in Ramseur, Randolph County, North Carolina.
10. John E. Albright (1839-1910) – Sergeant Co. C 10th NC Light Artillery was born in Randolph County where he resided as a farmer and enlisted at age 22, July 1, 1861 for the war. Mustered in as a private. Appointed sergeant November-December 1862. Present or accounted for through February 1865. Jordan, *Roster*, v. 1, 63. John was Catharine's brother. The last muster roll available on John is dated Jan/Feb 1865 and it states he was "Absent on detached service with horses since Nov. 21, 1864." That is why he was not at Appomattox to surrender. After the war, John was married and had five children. He is buried in the Shiloh Baptist Church Cemetery in Ramseur, Randolph County, North Carolina.

Notes

11. Matthew is referring to the Conscription Act of April 1862.
12. Thomas James Clegg (unknown-1862) – Captain Co. D 48th NC resided in Moore County. Elected 1st lieutenant on February 25, 1862. Promoted to captain on April 9, 1862. Wounded in the left thigh at King's School House, Virginia, June 25, 1862. Hospitalized at Richmond, Virginia, where he died on July 8-9, 1862, of wounds. [Previously served as captain in the 51st Regiment N. C. Militia.] Jordan, *Roster*, v. XI, 408.
13. The bounty for joining the Confederate army was fifty dollars.
14. Matthew often referred to two of his younger brothers, Isaac and Jones, as the boys.
15. William Nicholas Brower (1825-1905) was married to Matthew's sister, Amelia Yow (1834-1894). On the 1860 U.S. Census he is listed as a farmer in Moore County and in 1870 he is listed as a miller in Randolph County.
16. Likeness was the word used for photograph.
17. Simeon Jones Yow (1840-1900) – Corporal Co. D 15th NC previously served in Co. C, Mallett's Battalion (Camp Guard). Transferred to this company on or about April 7, 1863. Present or accounted for until wounded at Bristoe Station, Virginia, October 14, 1863. Reported absent wounded until he returned to duty on April 4, 1864. Promoted to corporal in May-August, 1864. Present or accounted for until reported absent without leave on August 24, 1864. Reported absent without leave through October, 1864. Jordan, *Roster*, v. V, 549. Matthew's brother, was known by his middle name, Jones. Jones was married after the war; he and his wife raised ten children in Randolph County where he farmed. He is buried in the Fair Grove Methodist Cemetery in Thomasville, Davidson County, North Carolina.
18. This refers to an infection.
19. Isaac Yow (1838-1906) – Private Co. D 15th NC resided in Moore County and enlisted at age 23, April 7, 1863, for the war. Present or accounted for until wounded at Bristoe Station, Virginia, October 14, 1863. Reported absent wounded until reported absent without leave on February 1, 1864. Reported absent without leave through October, 1864. [Company records indicate that he enlisted in Mallett's Battalion (Camp Guard) on July 18, 1862, and was transferred to this company on April 7, 1863; however, records of Mallett's Battalion do not indicate that he served therein.] Jordan, *Roster*, v. V, 549. Isaac was one of Matthew's brothers. He was married before the war; Isaac and his wife lived in Randolph County and had four children according to the 1880 census. He is buried in Liberty, Randolph County, North Carolina.
20. William Pool (1839-1864) – Private Co. D 48th NC was born in Randolph County and resided in Moore Couty where he was by occupation a farmer prior to enlisting in Moore County at age 22, February 25, 1862. Deserted on August 28, 1862. Returned to duty in March-April, 1863. Reported present in May-June, 1863. Hospitalized at Richmond, Virginia, April 12,

Notes

1864, with pneumonia. Died in hospital at Richmond on or about June 1, 1864, of "enteritis." Jordan, *Roster*, v. XI, 416. William was one of Matthew's neighbors.

21. Andrew J. Stutts (abt. 1832-1916) – Private Co. D 48th NC was born in Moore County where he resided as a farmer prior to enlisting in Moore County at age 33, March 13, 1862. Wounded in the right leg (fracture) at King's School House, Virginia, June 25, 1862. Right leg amputated. Reported absent wounded on surviving company muster rolls for the period from September, 1862, through October, 1864. [North Carolina pension records indicate that he survived the war.] Jordan, *Roster*, v. XI, 417. Andrew was probably Matthew's first cousin (the son of John Henry Stutts and Sarah E. Yow).

22. David D. Yow (1837-1896) – Private Co. D 48th NC was born in Moore County where he resided as a farmer prior to enlisting in Moore County at age 26, March 10, 1862. Discharged at Goldsboro on May 23, 1862. Reason discharged not reported. Jordan, *Roster*, v. XI, 419. David was Matthew's first cousin (son of Matthew Yow and Maloney Stutts Yow). David was married before the war began; after the war, they became the parents of eight children. He is buried at Flint Hill Baptist Church Cemetery in Robbins, Moore County, North Carolina.

23. James McPherson, *Battle Cry of Freedom: The Civil War Era* (New York: Oxford University Press, 1988), 487-488. For every soldier who died in combat two died of disease. The four most deadly diseases of the war were diarrhea/dysentery, typhoid, pneumonia, and malaria. Many regiments lost half their men to disease before even going into battle.

24. David D. Yow was discharged from the army on May 23, 1862.

25. Peter Moody is listed in the 1860 U. S. Census as a farmer. He and Matthew may have had a business connection since no familial link is known.

26. The Norfolk and Petersburg Railroad was completed in 1858. It was an important means of transporting ordnance to Norfolk during the early part of the war until the city fell to the Union army in the spring of 1862. Walkup wrote this assessment of the situation in his diary dated June 10-13, 1862, "We did a very foolish thing to destroy so much of the best railroad in the country I ever saw unnecessarily, for the Yankee had done the same thing on the Norfolk side and taken away the iron, so between friend and foe it is hard to tell from whom old Virginia suffered the most." Burpeau, *Writings of a Rebel Colonel*, 44-45.

27. Salt, needed for preserving meat, was becoming scarce.

28. The referenced letter of June 3 is not part of this collection. Catharine may not have received it.

29. This letter is a partial.

30. This refers to Catharine's brothers, John and Henry.

Notes

31. Matthew was part of a mission to obtain ice from the plantation home of Dr. Eppes, located on the James River, to be used at the NC hospital in Petersburg. The next morning, the Confederates attacked the enemy gun boats and were driven away by a counterattack. Lawhon wrote in his history of the regiment, "We went back to our camp having, as we thought, tasted a little of war and seen a little of its danger." Lawhon, "Forty-Eighth Regiment," 115.
32. The reference is to Major Benjamin R. Huske.
33. Christopher Columbus Harrison (1836-1865) – Private Co. H 26th NC resided in Moore County where he enlisted at age 25, July 1, 1861. Present or accounted for until wounded and captured at or near Gettysburg, Pennsylvania, July 1-5, 1863. Confined at David's Island, New York Harbor, July 17-24, 1863. Paroled at David's Island and transferred to City Point, Virginia, where he was received September 16, 1863 for exchange. Returned to duty in January-February, 1864. Present or accounted for until captured at or near Burgess' Mill, Virginia, October 27, 1864. Confined at Point Lookout, Maryland, where he died on February 14, 1865. Cause of death not reported. Jordan, *Roster*, v. VII, 565. Columbus was the son of Matthew's grandfather's second wife, Nancy Harrison Yow.
34. Matthew resumed his letter writing after attending preaching in camp. It is well documented by others that there was preaching every Sunday in camp. Walkup wrote in his journal about a Sunday sermon on July 13, 1862 (Burpeau, *Writings of a Rebel Colonel*, 55.). William A. Collins, private in Company C, wrote to his mother on July 21, 1862, from Camp Lee in Petersburg, "...I am thankful to God that we are blessed with the opportunity of having preaching in our regiment every Sunday..." ("William A. Collins Papers," Southern History Collection, Wilson Library, University of North Carolina, Chapel Hill, North Carolina).
35. Andrew Yow (1781-1869) was Matthew's grandfather.
36. Nancy (1807-1880) was Columbus' mother and Matthew's step-grandmother (married to Andrew Yow).

Chapter Two

1. 19th Century Naming Pattern Roots Web Ancestry.com. Retrieved on February 19, 2023 from https://homepages.rootsweb.com/~smalljd/smtbnp.html.
2. Kenneth W. Noe, *Reluctant Rebels: The Confederates Who Joined the Army after 1861* (Chapel Hill: The University of North Carolina Press, 2010), 84.
3. This was the opening of the Seven Days Battles fought near Richmond (June 25-July 1, 1862).

Notes

4. This reference is to the 4th Georgia Infantry Regiment. According to the article their action in the battle was "beyond all praise." "The Great Battle Renewed!" *Weekly Observer*, Fayetteville, North Carolina, June 30, 1862, 2.
5. Isaac Brady (abt. 1817-1862) – Private Co. D 48th NC was born in Randolph County and resided in Moore County where he was by occupation a farmer prior to enlisting in Moore County at age 45, March 8, 1862. "Kiled {sic} dead on the field" at King's School House, Virginia, June 25, 1862. Jordan, *Roster*, v. XI, 410.
6. This reference is to Captain Clegg. See note 12.
7. John H. Anderson (1839-unknown) – 1st lieutenant Co. D 48th NC previously served as corporal in Company H, 1st Regiment NC Infantry (6 months, 1861). Elected 3rd lieutenant of this company on February 24, 1862. Promoted to 2nd lieutenant on April 8, 1862. Wounded in the leg at King's School House, Virginia, June 25, 1862. Promoted to 1st lieutenant on June 28, 1862. Reported absent wounded in September-October, 1862. Resigned on November 14, 1862, by reason of disability from wounds. Resignation accepted on February 10, 1863. Later served as an enrolling officer in North Carolina. Jordan, *Roster*, v. XI, 408.
8. Major Benjamin R. Huske was wounded and later died on July 15, 1862. His wound was "at first supposed not to be dangerous, but erysipelas followed, of which he died." Jordan, *Roster*, v. XI, 369.
9. The 48th North Carolina was detached from Ransom's brigade and attached to Walker's brigade.
10. Colonel Hill was upset about the situation on the field of battle which resulted in many casualties; the regiment advanced across an open field to attack Federal forces in the woods behind a fence. Lawhon, "Forty-Eighth Regiment," 115.
11. John F. Williamson (1840-unknown) – Private Co. F 46th NC was born in Moore County where he resided as a farmer prior to enlisting in Randolph County at age 22, March 26, 1862, as a substitute. Present or accounted for until he deserted at Martinsburg, [West] Virginia, September 19, 1862. Returned from desertion on December 29, 1862. Sent to hospital at Petersburg, Virginia, January 8, 1863. Failed to return to duty and was dropped from the rolls of the company in May-June, 1864, because he was "supposed dead." Company muster roll dated July-August, 1864, states that he was "improperly enlisted [and was] sent to his company." No further records. Jordan, *Roster*, v. XI, 197.
12. Captain Thomas J. Clegg was wounded in the left thigh at King's School House and died on July 8-9, 1862. Jordan, *Roster*, v. XI, 408.
13. James C. Dowd (1835-1898) – Captain Co. D 48th NC resided in Moore County. Elected 2nd lieutenant on February 24, 1862. Promoted to 1st lieutenant on April 9, 1862. Promoted to captain on or about July 28, 1862. Wounded in the left foot at Fredericksburg, Virginia, December 13, 1862.

Notes

Resigned on an unspecified date by reason of "anchylosis" of the left foot resulting from wounds received at Fredericksburg. Resignation accepted on September 7, 1863. Jordan, *Roster*, v. XI, 408.

14. Matthew finally had his photograph taken in Petersburg after saying in other letters he was planning to do so.
15. Lewis Grant Maness (1816-1913) was the son of Matthew's great aunt, Sarah Yow Maness, and her husband, John Wesley Maness. On the 1860 U.S. Census he is listed as a Moore County farmer. He enlisted into the 6th NC Senior Reserves on July 2, 1864.
16. Matthew is referring to Catharine's two brothers.
17. Isaac Williams is listed on the 1860 U.S. Census as a farmer who lived close to Matthew.
18. Samuel D. Stewart (1830-1863) – 1st Sergeant Co. D 48th NC resided in Moore County where he enlisted at age 32, May 14, 1862, for the war. Mustered in as private. Promoted to 1st sergeant prior to September 17, 1862. Wounded and captured at Sharpsburg, Maryland, September 17, 1862. Paroled on or about September 27, 1862. Reported absent wounded in January-April, 1863. Died on or about May 1, 1863, of wounds. Place of death not reported. Jordan, *Roster*, v. XI, 417.
19. Matthew's brothers, Jones and Isaac, joined Colonel Mallett's Battalion about the end of July 1862.
20. This may be a midwife. Catharine was eight months pregnant and Matthew shows much concern about her well-being in this letter.
21. This reference is to the free Black population (mostly women) in Petersburg who were trying to make a living by selling pies and other sweet treats to the soldiers. See A. Wilson Greene, *Civil War Petersburg: Confederate City in the Crucible of War* (Charlottesville: University of Virginia Press, 2006), 124.
22. At the Battle of French's Farm, a Virginia regiment was expected to support the 48th on the right but never came up. The 48th NC fought an entire brigade of Federals before a Georgian battalion arrived thus enabling them to hold the ground. This may be what Matthew was thinking about while writing this letter. Lawhon, "Forty-Eighth Regiment," 115.
23. Matthew was referring to yellow fever, which is a viral disease spread by mosquitoes. It is characterized by jaundice and high fever. William Collins, a private in Co. C, wrote to his father on August 15, 1862, concerning this illness by describing it as a "right smart sickness now in camp, some fever and jaundice and other complaints." ("William A. Collins Papers").
24. The Second Battle of Manassas (Bull Run) was fought on August 29-30, 1862.
25. Matthew is referring to galluses which are suspenders for trousers.
26. The Battle of Fredericksburg occurred on December 13, 1862.
27. There was much opposition to the Confederacy in the central Piedmont region. Matthew may be referring to a group known as the Heroes of Amer-

Notes

ica, an organization composed of deserters and Unionists. There was ongoing violence between the group's members and loyal Confederates; barns were burned and crops were stolen just to name two violent acts occurring during that time. See Gordon B. McKinney, *Zeb Vance: North Carolina's Civil War Governor and Gilded Age Political Leader* (Chapel Hill: The University of North Carolina Press, 2004), 160.

28. Colonel Walkup's letter to Governor Vance dated Oct. 11, 1862, communicated the urgent needs of the regiment. Of the 619 men rank and file there were 51 men who were barefooted and 194 men who would be barefooted in less than a month. There were no tents and the 297 blankets had to be shared among all the men. S. H. Walkup Lt. Col. S. H. Walkup to Gov. Zebulon Vance, October 11, 1862, in the Governor's Papers, North Carolina State Archives, Raleigh, NC. See also Burpeau, *Writings of a Rebel Colonel*, 66.

29. This reference may be to Stanly County in N.C.

Chapter Three

1. George C. Rable, *God's Almost Chosen Peoples: A Religious History of the American Civil War* (Chapel Hill: The University of North Carolina Press, 1994), 9.
2. Confederate regiments were being sent to the coastal area due to the buildup of Union forces there. The Federal forces were assembled at Beaufort, North Carolina, to assist in a joint land and naval attack on the defenses of Wilmington. The attack did not occur. Barrett, *The Civil War in North Carolina*, 150n.
3. New Bern fell to the Union army in March 1862. Confederate efforts in 1863 and 1864 to recapture New Bern were unsuccessful.
4. John Henry Stutts (1803-1876) – Private Co. D 48th NC was born in Moore County where he resided as a farmer prior to enlisting in Moore County at age 55, March 12, 1862. Reported absent on duty at Petersburg, Virginia, in September-October, 1862. Wounded in the head at Fredericksburg, Virginia, December 13, 1862. Returned to duty prior to March 1, 1863. Reported present or accounted for in March-June, 1863, and March April, 1864. Reported absent without leave on October 22, 1864. Jordan, *Roster*, v. XI, 418. John was Matthew's uncle by marriage; he was married to Matthew's aunt, Sarah E. Yow.
5. General John Rogers Cooke (1833-1891) was promoted to brigadier general on November 1, 1862.
6. John Lewis Maness (1824-1910) – Private Co. A 27th NC enlisted in Wake County on April 1, 1864, for the war. Present or accounted for through February 1865; however, he was reported absent sick during most

Notes

of that period. Jordan, *Roster*, v. VIII, 15. John was a Moore County farmer married to Matthew's sister, Julia A. Yow.

7. James G. Morgan (1819-1892) – Private Co. D 48th NC was born in Moore County where he resided as a farmer prior to enlisting in Moore County at age 43, March 13, 1862. Wounded at Sharpsburg, Maryland, on or about September 17, 1862. Returned to duty prior to November 1, 1862. Reported present or accounted for in January-June, 1863, and March-April, 1864. Hospitalized at Richmond, Virginia, May 27, 1864, with an unspecified complaint and was transferred on June 9, 1864. Last reported in the records of this company on September 14, 1864. Jordan, *Roster*, v. XI, 415.

8. The letter dated February 8th is not part of this collection; perhaps Catharine did not receive it.

9. George B. Campbell (1840-1863) – Sergeant Co. D 48th NC was born in Moore County where he resided as a farmer prior to enlisting in Moore County at age 22, March 7, 1862. Mustered in as corporal. Wounded at Sharpsburg, Maryland, on or about September 17, 1862. Returned to duty prior to November 1, 1862. Reported present in January-June, 1863. Promoted to sergeant on August 1, 1863. Wounded at Bristoe Station, Virginia, October 14, 1863. Died at Culpeper Court House, Virginia, October 25, 1863, of wounds. Jordan, *Roster*, v. XI, 410.

10. John, Matthew's fifth child, would be almost six months at this point.

11. The letter dated February 24th is not part of this collection; perhaps Catharine did not receive it.

12. James Monroe Garner was a Moore County farmer who lived close to Matthew and his family.

13. Matthew deserted from the hospital in September 1862. He attempted to find his way home but was unsuccessful; he was arrested and sent back to camp. Matthew stated his intention in the letter which was to see his family and find someone to help sow the wheat. This type of desertion was known as "French leave." Matthew did not intend to stay at home. This is in contrast to other deserters who left the ranks and did not plan to return.

14. Henry Wesley Stutts (1832-1904) – Private Co. D 48th NC was born in Moore County where he resided as a farmer prior to enlisting in Moore County at age 32, March 7, 1862. Wounded in the hand at Sharpsburg, Maryland, September 17, 1862. Hospitalized at Richmond, Virginia. Detailed for duty as a hospital nurse at Richmond on October 17, 1862. Rejoined the company on January 30, 1863. Reported present or accounted for in February-June, 1863; March-April, 1864; and September-October, 1864. Captured at Hatcher's Run, Virginia, April 1, 1865. Confined at Point Lookout, Maryland, April 2, 1865. Released at Point Lookout on June 20, 1865, after taking the Oath of Allegiance. Jordan, *Roster*, v. XI, 418. Henry was Matthew's first cousin, the son of Sarah E. Yow (1813-1862) and John Henry Stutts (1803-1876).

Notes

15. Elizabeth R. Yow (1832-1908) was Matthew's stepmother; he called her mother or Betsy at times.
16. This appears to be a partial letter. It is probably part of the letter dated Feb. 27, 1863.
17. Henry may have contracted smallpox in the Richmond hospital after his wounding and capture at the battle of Antietam. There was a smallpox epidemic in Richmond at that time. He returned to camp on January 30, 1863. Some soldiers were vaccinated against the disease, more Union soldiers than Confederates. There was no cure for smallpox and the fatality rate was 20-40 percent. Doctors promoted good ventilation and a healthy diet. See Glenna Schroeder-Lein, *The Encyclopedia of Civil War Medicine* (Armonk, NY: M. E. Sharpe, Inc., 2008), 278-279.
18. This letter is addressed to Catharine's parents, Joseph Albright (1794-1876) and Nancy Whitsitt Albright (1799-1882).
19. This notation means the letter was received in the present month.
20. A letter dated March 17th is not part of this collection. Catharine may not have received it.
21. The Union navy commanded by Rear Admiral Samuel F. Du Pont attacked Fort Sumter on April 7, 1863. The Federals were unable to recapture the fort.
22. William Stockard Albright (1826-1864) – Private Co. D 11th NC Infantry was not in the army at this time. He enlisted in Burke County on June 27, 1864, for the war. Present or accounted for until wounded in the head near Petersburg, Virginia, October 1, 1864. Died in hospital at Richmond, Virginia, October 4, 1864, of wounds. Jordan, *Roster*, v. V, 41. William was Catharine's brother. He left behind a wife and four children. He is buried at the Hollywood Cemetery in Richmond, Virginia.
23. It is not known if this letter was received by Catharine since it is not part of this collection.
24. David Yow was probably visiting the troops since he had been discharged from the army due to illness.
25. Jones and Isaac were transferred from Colonel Mallett's Battalion at Camp Holmes to Company D of the 15th North Carolina on April 7, 1863. They were then in the same brigade as Matthew.

Chapter Four

1. McPherson, *Battle Cry of Freedom*, 694-95.
2. Richard Bardolph. "Inconstant Rebels: Desertion of North Carolina Troops in the Civil War," *North Carolina Historical Review* XLI (April, 1964): 163-189.
3. S. H. Walkup Lt. Col. S. H. Walkup to Gov. Zebulon Vance, October 11, 1862, in the Governor's Papers, North Carolina State Archives, Raleigh,

Notes

NC.

4. Ella Lonn, *Desertion During the Civil War* (1928; repr., Lincoln: University of Nebraska Press, 1998), 3-20.
5. W. K. Boyd, "William W. Holden: Part II - Secession and Peace Movement," in THE TRINITY COLLEGE HISTORICAL PAPERS. Series III [Durham, NC: Historical Society of Trinity College, 1899]: 69.
6. Catharine accompanied Matthew to the train depot in High Point, NC at the end of his furlough.
7. Matthew is referring to the area where his regiment fought the first day of the Seven Days Battles in June 1862. It is very close to where the Battle of Seven Pines was fought May 31- June 1, 1862.
8. According to the diary of Samuel H. Walkup, the bones may have been used to make rings. Walkup wrote on June 20, 1863, "Many North Carolinians are buried here, and more Yankees lie shallow and unburied, their bones are lying on the surface and many of our soldiers desecrate them by making rings from them." Burpeau, *Writings of a Rebel Colonel*, 98.
9. Walkup's diary entry dated June 20, 1863, records this same information. He wrote, "...awful desecration of the dead visible in skulls and other bones lying exposed on the surface, mostly Yankees, whether exhumed or never buried." Burpeau, *Writings of a Rebel Colonel*, 99.
10. Jones and Isaac were transferred to the 15th North Carolina, not Matthew's regiment and company.
11. Matthew is referring to the Second Battle of Winchester fought June 13-15, 1863. It was a Confederate victory and the beginning of the Gettysburg Campaign.
12. Cooke's Brigade and others remained in the vicinity of Richmond while the majority of Lee's army fought at Gettysburg. Between July 1-7 the Federals under General Dix advanced from White House, VA toward Richmond. On July 3rd the Battle at Bottoms Bridge drove the enemy back toward White House. A few days later, the 27th and 48th regiments were stationed near the South Anna River Bridge to guard the way to Richmond.
13. This is a continuation of the letter to Catharine and the children dated July 3, 1863. At the bottom of the last page is written a short note to Matthew's step-mother.
14. Henry Maness, as Matthew wrote, was the brother of Elizabeth Maness Yow. He was in Co. A of Holcombe's Legion (cavalry) of South Carolina. The legion was in Richmond bolstering the city's defenses while other regiments were in Pennsylvania fighting the Battle of Gettysburg. In 1864, the cavalry units of Holcombe's Legion became part of the 7th SC Cavalry Regiment.
15. The reference may be to Hiram Williamson, listed in the 1860 U.S. Census as a farmer that lived very close to Matthew and his family. Here he is suspected of killing the boar. In a future letter he will be suspected of killing a sow.

Notes

16. A tory was a term for a Southerner that was a Union sympathizer.
17. David Williamson lived next door to Matthew's family according to the 1860 U.S. Census and was listed as a farmer. It is not known what Matthew was referring to.
18. It is not known what is being referenced. Could Catharine have been receiving some form of aid from the government or earning money for a service she is providing such as sewing? Some letters mention thread, needles, and pins. It could be that Catharine had a job as a seamstress. Many women in the South during the war worked an extra job out of necessity. In addition to maintaining the home and managing the farm, Catharine did all she could to provide for her family. See Faust, *Mothers of Invention*, 80-113.
19. Confederate forces under General Matt Ransom repulsed Union forces led by Colonel Samuel P. Spear and General John G. Foster on July 28, 1863, trying to destroy the railroad bridge at Weldon, NC. Known as the Boone's Mill Fight, the Confederate victory allowed the Wilmington and Weldon Railroad to keep supplying the Army of Northern Virginia. Barrett, *The Civil War in North Carolina*, 166-170.
20. This letter to Catharine is a partial and was written between July 4 and August 15, 1863.
21. Matthew is referring to the Battle of Gettysburg fought July 1-3, 1863.
22. Cornelius Alexander Stutts (1840-1869) – Private Co. D 48th NC resided in Moore County where he enlisted at age 23, April 28, 1862, for the war. Deserted on August 22, 1862. Returned to duty on February 9, 1863. Reported present in March-June, 1863; March-April, 1864; and September-October, 1864. Captured near Petersburg, Virginia, April 2, 1865. Confined at Point Lookout, Maryland, April 5, 1865. Released at Point Lookout on June 20, 1865, after taking the Oath of Allegiance. *Roster*, v. XI, 417. Cornelius was married to Matthew's first cousin, Lydia J. Yow.
23. Wiat Williamson was a Moore County farmer according to the 1860 U.S. census. He lived close to Matthew.
24. Matthew is referring to the Battle of Gettysburg.
25. According to George C. Rable from the book *God's Almost Chosen Peoples* page 73, "Ministers searched for Old Testament parallels to contemporary events that could somehow propel the Confederate States of America into a larger providential history." It seems that Matthew is applying what he has read or heard preached to the current days.
26. There is no date on this letter to Henry. It may have been written in August of 1863.
27. There is no date on this letter to Nancy and Jane. It may have been written in August of 1863.
28. This letter has three dates (August 21, 23, and 24) but was written on one piece of paper.

Notes

29. August 21, 1863, was one of many days that were set apart by the Confederate president, Jefferson Davis, for fasting, humiliation, and prayer.
30. Reuben Maness (1836-1864) – Private Co. G 46th NC was born in Moore County and resided in Randolph County where he was by occupation a teacher prior to enlisting in Randolph County at age 26, March 25, 1862. Present or accounted for through June, 1864. Wounded near Petersburg, Virginia, on an unspecified date. Died on August 11, 1864, of wounds. Place of death not reported. Jordan, *Roster*, v. XI, 215.
31. Matthew was concerned about the way the Confederate leaders violated the Sabbath Day. Other Confederate soldiers wrote home with the same concern. Noe. *Reluctant Rebels*, 146.
32. This could possibly be referring to a home guard group. Such groups of men rounded up deserters and attempted to maintain law and order in communities. They were not always trusted. Sometimes they participated in lawlessness.

Chapter Five

1. McPherson, *Battle Cry of Freedom*, 440
2. McPherson, *Battle Cry of Freedom*, 440
3. The bread riots in the spring of 1863 occurred in about a dozen cities throughout the South including Raleigh, Atlanta, and Richmond. They were led by women who were upset about inflation and tired of seeing their children go hungry. McPherson, *Battle Cry of Freedom*, 617-18.
4. *The Civil War: A Visual History* (Dorling Kindersley, 2011) 199.
5. Bruce Catton, *The Civil War* (1960; repr., Boston: Houghton Mifflin Company, 2004), 170.
6. It is not known from whom Catharine was receiving money. See Chapter Four, note #18.
7. A merchant named Eli N. Moffit lived near Matthew according to the 1860 U.S. Census.
8. Matthew is referring to the second of two prolonged revivals that swept through the Army of Northern Virginia. The first was along the Rappahannock River in the area of Fredericksburg, Virginia from September 1862 until May 1863. Matthew's reference is to the revival that occurred from August 1863 until May 1864 mostly along the Rapidan River near Orange Court House, Virginia. During both periods large numbers of soldiers professed their Christian faith and some were baptized. Refer to Troy C. Harman, *The Great Revival of 1863: The Effects Upon Lee's Army of Northern Virginia* (Penny Hill Press, 2013).
9. After a sermon was preached the men were invited to come forward to repent of their sins and inquire about salvation. The soldiers were referred to as mourners. Refer to Andrew Scott Bledsoe. "We are a Spectacle to

Notes

God": The Phenomenon of Confederate Revivalism. Academic Forum 23. 2005-06. www.hsu.edu. Pages 37-59.

10. David S. Fairley (1831-1912) was chaplain of the 27th North Carolina Regiment. He resided in Cumberland County. Appointed chaplain on February 10, 1863. Resigned on or about December 8, 1863. Reason he resigned not reported. Jordan, *Roster*, v. VIII, 9.

11. Samuel W. Howerton (unknown) was chaplain of the 15th North Carolina Regiment. Resided in Davidson County. Appointed chaplain on April 10, 1865, to rank from February 24, 1863. Present or accounted for until he resigned on December 10, 1864. Jordan, *Roster*, v. V, 503.

12. Charles Carroll Dodson (1832-1884) was chaplain of the 46th North Carolina Regiment. He was Methodist, born in 1832, and resided in Davidson County. Appointed chaplain on May 31, 1863. Resigned on October 31, 1864, by reason of physical disability. Jordan, *Roster*, v. XI, 135.

13. Calvin Plyler (1828-1910) was chaplain of the 48th North Carolina Regiment. Methodist-Episcopal. Resided in Iredell County and enlisted at age 33. Appointed chaplain on September 21, 1863. Present or accounted for through February, 1865. Jordan, *Roster*, v. XI, 370.

14. Scarlet fever was a deadly bacterial illness that led to many childhood deaths during the 1800s. It would usually start with a sore throat and high fever. Matthew was probably aware that General Longstreet and his wife lost three children (Augustus, Jane, and Mary Anne) to scarlet fever in January and February of 1862.

15. William Woods Holden (1818-1892) was the owner and editor of the *North Carolina Standard* in Raleigh.

16. Zebulon B. Vance (1830-1894) was the governor of North Carolina at this time.

17. Sam Christian ran against Thomas S. Ashe for a seat in the Confederate Congress (7th NC District) and lost shortly after the date of this letter.

18. Levi Wright (1814-unknown) – Private Co. D 48th NC was born in Moore County where he resided as a mechanic prior to enlisting in Moore County at age 46, March 13, 1862. Reported absent sick in September-October, 1862, and January-February, 1863. Reported present in March-June, 1863. Captured at Bristoe Station, Virginia, October 14, 1863. Confined at Old Capitol Prison, Washington, D. C. Transferred to Point Lookout, Maryland, October 27, 1863. Paroled at Point Lookout on or about March 16, 1864. Received at City Point, Virginia, March 20, 1864, for exchange. Reported absent without leave on August 1, 1864. Jordan, *Roster*, v. XI, 419.

19. James Wright, Levi's son, was about 17 years old at this time. He was not enlisted in the army.

20. John N. Rich (1844-1903) – Private Co. C 10th NC Light Artillery enlisted in Lenoir County March 2, 1863 for the war. Present or accounted

Notes

for through February 1865. Jordan, *Roster*, v. 1, 71. John Rich was the son of Catharine's sister, Jane Albright.

21. Thomas Craven (1832-1893) was the husband of Catharine's sister, Mary Eleanor Albright. He was listed in the 1860 U.S. Census as living in Randolph County. He was 35 years old in 1860 and his occupation was listed as a Christian minister.
22. This may be B. F. Coffin who is listed on the 1860 U.S. Census as a 45-year-old Randolph County farmer. Dorset could not be identified.
23. Captured deserters were being sent back to their regiments. In September under the direction of Gov. Vance, General Robert F. Hoke and a regiment of Confederate troops rounded up about three thousand deserters and conscripts hiding out in the central and western counties of the state. During the month of October about two thousand troops returned to their regiments. McKinney, *Zeb Vance*, 189.
24. The Battle of Bristoe Station was a debacle for the Confederates. A. P. Hill had failed to reconnoiter the area and sent two of Heth's brigades (Cooke's and Kirkland's) into the fight against overwhelming odds.
25. This is a partial letter written after the Battle of Bristoe Station in October 1863.
26. William and Horner have not been identified.
27. This person could be Doctor John Shaw or an officer named Charles Shaw in Co. D of the 48th NC.
28. Reference is to Levi Wright.
29. Graham's Battery was Company C of the 10th North Carolina Light Artillery Regiment. Henry and John Albright were in this battery.
30. Walkup wrote in a letter to Gov. Vance dated Nov. 13, 1863, "Ours and Kirkland's Brigades were shamefully sacrificed at Bristoe Station." Burpeau, *Writings of a Rebel Colonel*, 108.
31. Matthew is stating the losses of Company D.
32. Cooke's brigade lost about this number in men that were killed, wounded, and captured out of 2,500 that were engaged in the fighting. Kirkland's brigade lost about 600 men out of 1,500.
33. General Henry Heth (1825-1899) was the division commander under A. P. Hill. Hill accepted blame for the mismanagement of the battle. Matthew may have been referring to General Heth's involvement in precipitating the Battle of Gettysburg on July 1, 1863, before the entire Confederate army was present.
34. General John Rogers Cooke was seriously injured in the shin. It was thought that he died on the field. After months of recovery, he returned to the army in Spring 1864 with his leg intact.
35. Colonel Edward D. Hall, of the 46th North Carolina, assumed command of Cooke's brigade.
36. Columbus is mentioned four times in the letters (Nov. '63 – Mar. '64). There is a possibility that the reference is to Christopher Columbus

Notes

37. Harrison whose muster rolls would support the possibility.
37. This reference is to Sarah, Matthew's sister that was born in 1838.
38. This partial was written during the winter of 1863/1864.
39. The first part of this letter is missing and the second part is torn and missing much content. It was written to Catharine after October 14, 1863.
40. Matthew is probably referring to the home guard or another group that is hunting for deserters and draft dodgers.
41. George Moore was a Moore County farmer listed on the 1860 U.S. Census. He was 37 years old in 1860. He lived close to Matthew's family.
42. There were several men by this name in Moore County. It can't be known if this was John F. Williamson or another John Williamson in the county.

Chapter Six

1. William S. Powell, "John Rogers Cooke," *Dictionary of North Carolina Biography* (Chapel Hill: University of North Carolina Press, 1996), online at ncpedia.org.
2. Mrs. Pool could be the wife or mother of William Pool.
3. James Hunsucker (1821-1895) – Private Co. D 48th NC was born in Moore County where he resided as a mechanic prior to enlisting in Moore County at age 40, February 26, 1862. Mustered in as private. Promoted to corporal on an unspecified date. Reduced to ranks on September 7, 1862. Reported present but under arrest for desertion in September-October, 1862. Reported absent sick in May-June, 1863. Returned to duty on an unspecified date. Reported present in March-April and September-October, 1864. Wounded at Hatcher's Run, Virginia, February 5, 1865. Deserted to the enemy on or about March 24, 1865. Confined at Washington, D.C., March 29, 1865. Released on an unspecified date after taking the Oath of Allegiance. *Roster*, v. XI, 413.
4. This Dorcas may be the wife of Isaac Yow, Susannah Dorcas Maness Yow (1840-1906).
5. Carter has not been identified.
6. The Southern Express Company advertised services to ship packages to the soldiers from certain cities. In North Carolina, Catharine would need to get a package to Raleigh to be shipped to Richmond, Virginia. From there packages were delivered to the soldiers. Raleigh was about 70 miles from Catharine's home near Robbins.
7. John Crisco (1817-1897) was a 41-year-old Moore County farmer according to the 1860 U.S. census. He joined the 6th NC Senior Reserves in December 1864.
8. Augustine Crouch (1839-1864) – Private Co. K 48th NC was born in Forsyth County and resided in Davidson County where he was by occupation a planter prior to enlisting in Forsyth County at age 23, March 20,

Notes

1862. Wounded at Sharpsburg, Maryland, on or about September 17, 1862. Returned to duty prior to March 1, 1863. Reported present in March-April, 1863. Deserted on or about May 5, 1863. Reported at home on sick furlough in January-April, 1864. No further records. *Roster*, v. XI, 487. Walkup, in his diary entry dated January 25, 1864, says Augustine was executed for desertion. Burpeau, *Writings of a Rebel Colonel*, 118.

9. Dr. John Shaw (1824-1898) was a Moore County physician.
10. Betsy was Matthew's stepmother.
11. This is a letter to Joseph Albright. It is torn and missing much content. Much of it is rubbed or washed out.
12. It seems that Mr. Albright sent the Oath of Allegiance to Matthew probably as an insult. In early December 1863, President Lincoln issued the Ten Percent Plan (the Proclamation of Amnesty and Reconstruction) to help reunite the nation. Confederate states would be permitted to rejoin the Union when ten percent of its voters swore an oath of allegiance to the Constitution. Anyone who took the oath had to accept the abolition of slavery to receive the benefits of the full pardon. This was not a popular plan among Southerners or abolitionists. See www.whitehousehistory.org. Also see Donald, *Lincoln*, 471-72.
13. The soldiers of Lee's army along the Rapidan River were hungry most of the time during the winter of 1863-64. They were often on short rations. Lee issued a general order during that time informing the men that he was working to procure needed food and other supplies. See Capt. Robert Edward Lee, *Recollections and Letters of Robert E. Lee* (Mineola, New York: Dover Publications, Inc., 2007), 118-119.
14. Matthew may be referring to Isaiah 8:12 (KJV) which reads, "Say ye not, A confederacy, to all them to whom this people shall say, A confederacy; neither fear ye their fear, nor be afraid."
15. It was believed by some that during the Revolutionary War "...the American Patriot cause seemed more hopeless than the Confederate situation did in August 1863." This observation made by Governor Vance and others was meant to give the soldiers encouragement to fight on. McKinney, *Zeb Vance*, 180.
16. Youtha Ann Albright (1834-1913) was one of Catharine's sisters.
17. This last mention of an unidentified Columbus gives us the clue that he was a deserter. It is not known if he was Christopher Columbus Harrison or another Columbus.
18. People were beginning to associate contaminated water with deadly camp diseases such as dysentery and typhoid fever.
19. Governor Vance visited the troops in camp as part of his reelection campaign. On March 30th, he addressed the brigades of Cooke and Kirkland. Samuel Walkup wrote in his journal afterwards, "He made a good Vance speech, but it was scarcely dignified enough for the Governor of

Notes

North Carolina before Generals J.E.B. Stuart, Heth and others of our own state." Burpeau, *Writings of a Rebel Colonel*, 127.

Many soldiers did not like the statement Vance made about fighting until Hell freezes over. He later denied having said the expression but some soldiers made it known that the governor was not being truthful. One such soldier was Matthew's cousin-in-law, C. A. Stutts, who wrote a letter to the editor of a Raleigh newspaper in July 1864, exposing Vance's lie. "Gov. Vance's Army Speeches," *The Daily Progress* (Raleigh, NC), 30 July 1864, page 2.

20. Montraville D. Clegg (1841-1864) was born in Chatham County where he resided as a student prior to enlisting in Moore County at the age of 21, March 3, 1862. He mustered in as first sergeant. After several promotions he became 1st lieutenant on September 7, 1863. He was wounded at Cold Harbor, Virginia, on June 3, 1864. He returned to duty prior to August 25, 1864, when he was killed at Reams Station, Virginia. Jordan, *Roster*, v. XI, 408.

Chapter Seven

1. Matthew wrote his last letter home (that is in this collection) on the same day that Colonel Walkup wrote in his diary and described the weather. Walkup wrote, "Rain, snow, sleet, followed by hard wind." Burpeau, *Writings of a Rebel Colonel*, 128.
2. Union forces numbered approximately 102,000 and Confederate forces about 61,000. *The Wilderness*. American Battlefield Trust. Retrieved on July 21, 2022, from https://www.battlefields.org/learn/civil-war/battles/wilderness. Grant had an advantage in numbers but was at a disadvantage with his cavalry and artillery since they could not function well in the tangled undergrowth.
3. The Germanna/Brock Road ran 15 miles south from the Rapidan River to Spotsylvania Court House, Virginia. It intersected with Orange Plank Road and the Orange Turnpike, strategic locations that both armies sought to control.
4. Jordan, *North Carolina Troops*, v. XI, 132.
5. Lawhon, "Forty-Eighth Regiment," 118.
6. Heth and Wilcox (two of the three third corps division commanders) asked General Hill after the fighting ceased on May 5th to allow them to straighten their lines to prepare for the next day. Hill replied that Lee did not want the men disturbed because Longstreet would arrive soon to take their place at the front. See Gordon C. Rhea, *The Battle of the Wilderness: May 5-6, 1864* (Baton Rouge: Louisiana State University Press, 2000), 276-277.
7. Wheelen, *Bloody Spring*, 99.

Notes

8. Anderson's Division of the Third Corps had been left behind to guard the Rapidan River. They were now being called into battle with Longstreet's First Corps.
9. The number of men wounded, missing, or killed was estimated to be 29,800 after the second day of battle. The Union casualties were approximately 17,000 and the Confederate casualties approximately 13,000. *The Wilderness*. American Battlefield Trust. Retrieved on July 21, 2022, from https://www.battlefields.org/learn/civil-war/battles/wilderness
10. From the unpublished letters of Henry A. Albright in the possession of Larry R. Yow.
11. Horace Porter, *Campaigning with Grant* (New York: Century Co., 1897), 72-73.
12. Lawhon, "Forty-Eighth Regiment," 119.
13. Thomas, *History of the Doles-Cook Brigade*, 479.
14. An area of land in the northwestern part of the Rebel fortifications not easily protected due to the way it jutted out (salient). It was a necessary part of the fortifications because it was on high ground.
15. Lawhon, "Forty-Eighth Regiment," 119.
16. From the May 16, 1864 diary entry of Walkup. Burpeau, *Writings of a Rebel Colonel*, 137.
17. The battle around Spotsylvania Court House lasted for 12 days and the casualties numbered more than 30,000. The number of Union troops wounded, missing, or killed was 18,399 and for the Confederates, 12,687. *Spotsylvania Court House*. American Battlefield Trust. Retrieved July 21, 2022, from https://www.battlefields.org/learn/civil-war/battles/spotsylvania-court-house
18. General A. P. Hill had recovered from his illness and was again in command of the Third Corps.
19. Hanover Junction was a small town with a busy railroad intersection. The Richmond, Fredericksburg, and Potomac Railroad ran north and south connecting Richmond with northern Virginia. It transported food, ammunition, and supplies to the soldiers and transported the wounded to Richmond. It intersected with the Central Virginia Railroad that brought in supplies from the Shenandoah Valley. Protecting Hanover Junction was vitally important for the Confederate army. Mackowski, *Strike Them a Blow*, 51.
20. Lawhon, "Forty-Eighth Regiment," 119.
21. William Henry Harrison Lawhon (1841-1926) - Captain Co. D 48th NC resided in Moore County where he was a student prior to enlisting at age 20, February 25, 1862. Mustered in as sergeant. He was eventually promoted to captain on September 7, 1863. Surrendered at Appomattox Court House, Virginia, April 9, 1865. Jordan, *Roster*, v. XI, 408. W. H. H. Lawhon was the fourth captain of Company D and the only one not mentioned by Matthew in his letters.

Notes

22. Cornelius D. Lawhon (1834-1864) – 1st Sergeant Co. D 48th NC resided in Moore County where he enlisted at age 29, May 14, 1862, for the war. Mustered in as private. Reported present in September-October, 1862, and January-June, 1863. Promoted to sergeant in May-June, 1863. Reported present in March-April, 1864. Promoted to 1st sergeant prior to May 1, 1864. Killed at the North Anna River, near Hanover Junction, Virginia, on or about May 23, 1864, by the same cannon ball that mortally wounded Corporal Matthew C. Yow of this company. Jordan, *Roster*, v. XI, 413. Cornelius was the brother of Captain Lawhon.
23. On the muster roll dated Mar/Apr 1864, Matthew was listed as corporal.
24. Lawhon, "Forty-Eighth Regiment," 119.
25. Burpeau, *Writings of a Rebel Colonel*, 138.
26. *Semi-Weekly Observer*, Fayetteville, North Carolina, November 10, 1864, 2.
27. The date of Matthew's mortal wounding was recorded as May 25, 1864, in the regimental history written by W. H. H. Lawhon in 1901. Editing of Lawhon's history has changed the date to May 23rd. In Matthew's Bible the date is May 23rd and the letter from Lawhon to Catharine indicated that the wounding occurred on May 23rd. According to *Civil War Soldier Records and Profiles, 1861-1865*, Matthew mustered out on June 15, 1864, at Petersburg, Virginia. This supports Catharine's claim that Matthew was taken to Petersburg although we are certain he died before June 15, 1864.
28. This is a transcription error that Catharine made. The day before yesterday would be May 23, 1864.
29. "Loss became commonplace." By the end of the war, Catharine would mourn the death of her husband, a brother, and a brother-in-law. See Drew Gilpin Faust, *This Republic of Suffering: Death and the American Civil War* (New York: Vintage Civil War Library, 2009), xiii.
30. Many soldiers, including Matthew C. Yow, prepared their families for the possibility of their deaths through writing. Matthew's letters gave assurance to Catharine and other loved ones that he died a Good Death; he would surely meet them in heaven where they would part no more. See Drew Gilpin Faust, *This Republic of Suffering*, 3-31.
31. Blandford Cemetery. Petersburg, Virginia. Retrieved August 1, 2022, from: https://www.petersburgva.gov/303/Blandford-Cemetery. The majority of the soldiers buried at the cemetery were unknown. Only 3,700 names appear on the roster.
32. Lee's engineer, Martin L. Smith, designed the inverted V formation. It was based on the geography at the North Anna River. The design forced Grant's army into three parts and neither part could reinforce the other without recrossing the river. This provided good defense. As an offensive tool, Lee could quickly shuttle his troops around.
33. Mackowski, *Strike Them a Blow*, 114.
34. Burpeau, *Writings of a Rebel Colonel*, 140.

Notes

35. Lawhon, "Forty-Eighth Regiment," 120.
36. Captain Lawhon gave a horrific description of the battle in his regimental history. He wrote in reference to the Union troops, "One line would fire and fall down, another step over, fire and fall down, each line getting nearer us...but finding themselves cut to pieces so badly, they fell back in a little disorder." As the Federal troops retreated the men of the 48th rose all at once, gave a rebel yell, and "...poured lead into them." Lawhon, "Forty-Eighth Regiment," 120.
37. Union troops wounded, missing, or killed during the Cold Harbor battle was 12,737; Confederate troops numbered 4,595. *Cold Harbor Battlefield*. American Battlefield Trust. Retrieved on April 29, 2023 from https://www.battlefields.org/visit/battlefields/cold-harbor-battlefield.
38. Lawhon, "Forty-Eighth Regiment," 121.
39. The Federal forces under the leadership of Burnside had created a mine underneath Rebel lines and exploded it. Lee's soldiers were able to recover and seal off the breach. However, the Union army suffered the most from this debacle including the loss of many colored troops.
40. Burpeau, *Writings of a Rebel Colonel*, 152.
41. Confederate casualties were between 2,700 and 4,000. Greene, *Civil War Petersburg*, 238.
42. Burpeau, *Writings of a Rebel Colonel*, 160.
43. Lawhon, "Forty-Eighth Regiment," 122.
44. Jordan, *North Carolina Troops v. XI*, 368.
45. Lawhon, "Forty-Eighth Regiment", 123.
46. McCaslin, *Portraits of Conflict*, 42.

Appendix A

1. Information from the 1860 U.S. Census. The National Archives in Washington D.C.; Record Group: *Records of the Bureau of the Census*; Record Group Number: 29; Series Number: *M653*; Residence Date: *1860*; Home in 1860: *Stockton, Portage, Wisconsin*; Roll: *M653_1426*; Page: 379; Family History Library Film: 805426
2. Michael Shortell. *Roster of Wisconsin Volunteers: War of the Rebellion*. U.S., Civil War Soldier Records and Profiles, 1861-1865.
3. This brigade, composed of western regiments (one Indiana and three Wisconsin), was considered one of the best units in the U.S. Army. The Iron Brigade suffered the highest casualty rate during the war. McPherson, *Battle Cry of Freedom*, 528.
4. *North Anna May 23-26, 1864*. American Battlefield Trust. Retrieved on September 2, 2022 from: https://www.battlefields.org/learn/civil-war/battles/north-anna.

Notes

5. James Fallows. *The Blue and the Gray*. March 25, 2015. Retrieved on September 2, 2022 from: https://www.theatlantic.com/national/archive/2015/03/the-blue-and-the-gray/388511/.

Appendix B

1. Information about each soldier was compiled using muster rolls and other primary records such as North Carolina adjutant general's Roll of Honor, discharge certificates, medical records, prisoner of war records, newspaper casualty lists, and pension applications. Secondary sources used were post-war rosters and histories, cemetery records, and records of the United Daughters of the Confederacy. Jordan, *Roster*, 408.
2. No company rolls were located for May 1-August 31, 1862; November 1-December 31, 1862; July 1, 1863-February 29, 1864; May 1-August 31, 1864; or for the period after October 31, 1864. Jordan, *Roster*, 408.
3. The men of the unit that deserted to the enemy and became captive were not counted as casualties unless they met the criteria of being a casualty due to wounding or death.
4. Lawhon, "Forty-Eighth Regiment", 124.

Appendix C

1. McCaslin, *Portraits of Conflict*, 42. Thirty percent of the North Carolina troops did not return from the war.
2. Faust, *This Republic of Suffering*, xi. Faust explains her statement that "...one in five white southern men of military age did not survive the Civil War" in a chapter note. She discusses the ongoing conversations that historians have concerning the overall death rate of Confederate soldiers and that it could be "closer to one in four rather than one in five."
3. Jesse Brown (1839-1863) – Private Co. H 26th NC resided in Moore County where he enlisted on March 11, 1862. Present or accounted for until he was wounded mortally at Gettysburg, Pennsylvania, July 1, 1863. Died at Gettysburg on an unspecified date. Jordan, *Roster*, v. VII, 562. Jesse was married to Matthew's sister, Mary Elizabeth.
4. Lawrence M. Ward (1834-1864) – Private Co. F 24th NC resided in Randolph County where he enlisted at age 28, July 21, 1862, for the war. Present or accounted for until captured near Petersburg, Virginia, June 17, 1864. Confined at Point Lookout, Maryland, until transferred to Elmira, New York, July 27, 1864. Died at Elmira on December 10, 1864, of "congestion of the brain." Jordan, Roster, v. VII, 310. Lawrence was the husband of Catharine's sister, Rachel Albright Ward. They had one

Notes

daughter before he went off to war. Lawrence is buried at the Woodlawn National Cemetery in Elmira, New York.

Bibliography

MANUSCRIPTS AND PUBLIC RECORDS
William A. Collins Papers. Southern History Collection, Wilson Library, University of North Carolina, Chapel Hill, North Carolina.
1850 U.S. Federal Census
1860 U.S. Federal Census
1870 U.S. Federal Census
1880 U.S. Federal Census
1900 U.S. Federal Census

WEBSITES
American Battlefield Trust.com
Ancestry.com
Fold3.com
Findagrave.com
NCpedia.org

NEWSPAPERS
Fayetteville Semi-Weekly Observer, Fayetteville, North Carolina
Fayetteville Weekly Observer, Fayetteville, North Carolina
The Daily Progress, Raleigh, North Carolina

BOOKS AND ARTICLES
Bardolph, Richard. "Inconstant Rebels: Desertion of North Carolina Troops in the Civil War." *North Carolina Historical Review*. XLI (April, 1964): 163-189.
Barrett, John G. *The Civil War in North Carolina*. Chapel Hill: The University of North Carolina Press, 1963.
Bearss, Edwin C. *Fields of Honor: Pivotal Battles of the Civil War*. Washington, D.C.: National Geographic, 2006.
Bledsoe, Andrew Scott. "We are a Spectacle to God": The Phenomenon of Confederate Revivalism. *Academic Forum* 23. 2005-06. 37-59. www.hsu.edu.
Burpeau, Kemp. *Writings of a Rebel Colonel: The Civil War Diary and Letters of*

Bibliography

Samuel Walkup, 48th North Carolina Infantry. Jefferson, NC: McFarland, 2021.

Catton, Bruce. *The Civil War.* Boston: Houghton Mifflin Company, 1960.

Clark, Walter. *Histories of the Several Regiments and Battalions from North Carolina in the Great War, 1861-1865.* Goldsboro: Nash Brothers, 1901.

Crute, Joseph H., Jr. *Units of the Confederate States Army.* Midlothian, VA: Derwent Books, 1987.

Donald, David Herbert. *Lincoln.* New York: Simon & Schuster, 1995.

Dunkerly, R. M., Pfanz, D. C., and Ruth, D. R. *No Turning Back: A Guide to the 1864 Overland Campaign From the Wilderness to Cold Harbor, May 4- June 13, 1864.* California: Savas Beatie, 2014.

Faust, Drew Gilpin. *This Republic of Suffering: Death and the American Civil War.* New York: Vintage, 2009.

Faust, Drew Gilpin. *Mothers of Invention: Women of the Slaveholding South in the American Civil War.* Chapel Hill: University of North Carolina Press, 1996.

Finch, Francis M. *The Blue and the Gray and Other Verses.* New York: Henry Holt and Company, 1909.

Foote, Shelby. *The Civil War: A Narrative.* Volume 3: *Red River to Appomattox.* New York: Vintage Books, 1986. First published 1974.

Greene, A. Wilson. *Civil War Petersburg: Confederate City in the Crucible of War.* Charlottesville: University of Virginia Press, 2006.

Hardy, Michael C. *North Carolina in the Civil War.* Charleston: The History Press, 2011.

Harman, Troy, D. *The Great Revival of 1863: The Effects Upon Lee's Army of Northern Virginia.* Penny Lee Press, Inc., 2013.

Jordan, Weymouth T. *North Carolina Troops, 1861-1865: A Roster.* Raleigh: North Carolina Office of Archives and History, 1987.

Lawhon, W. H. *Forty-Eight Regiment.* Ed. Walter Clark. *Histories of the Several Regiments and Battalions from North Carolina in the Great War, 1861-1865.* Goldsboro: Nash Brothers, 1901.

Lee, Robert Edward (Capt.). *Recollections and Letters of Robert E. Lee.* Mineola, New York: Dover Publications, Inc. 2007.

Lonn, Ella. *Desertion in the Civil War.* Lincoln: University of Nebraska Press, 1998.

Mackowski, Chris. *Strike Them a Blow: Battle along the North Anna River, May 21-25,1864.* El Dorado Hills: Savas Beatie, 2015.

McCaslin, Richard B. Portraits of Conflict: *A Photographic History of North Carolina in the Civil War.* Fayetteville: The University of Arkansas Press, 1997.

Bibliography

McKinney, Gordon B. *Zeb Vance: North Carolina's Civil War Governor and Gilded Age Political Leader*. Chapel Hill: The University of North Carolina Press, 2004.

McPherson, James. *Battle Cry of Freedom: The Civil War Era*. New York: The Oxford Press, 1988.

Miller, J. Michael. *The North Anna Campaign: "Even To Hell Itself" May 21-26, 1864*. Lynchburg: H. E. Howard, Inc., 1989.

Noe, Kenneth W. *Reluctant Rebels: The Confederates Who Joined the Army after 1861*. Chapel Hill: The University of North Carolina Press, 2010.

Porter, Horace. *Campaigning with Grant*. New York: Century Co., 1897.

Rable, George C. *God's Almost Chosen Peoples: A Religious History of the American Civil War*. Chapel Hill: The University of North Carolina Press, 2010.

Rhea, Gordon C. *The Battle of the Wilderness: May 5-6, 1864*. Baton Rouge: Louisiana State University Press, 1994.

Rhea, Gordon C. *To the North Anna River: Grant and Lee, May 13-25, 1864*. Baton Rouge: Louisiana State University Press, 2000.

Schroeder-Lein, Glenna. *The Encyclopedia of Civil War Medicine*. Armonk, NY: M.E. Sharpe, Inc., 2008.

Shattuck, Gardiner H. *A Shield and Hiding Place: The Religious Life of the Civil War Armies*. Macon, GA: Mercer University Press, 1987.

Smithsonian. *The Civil War: A Visual History*. New York: Dorling Kindersley, 2015.

Thomas, Henry W. (Henry Walter). *History of the Doles-Cook Brigade of Northern Virginia, CSA.: Containing Muster Roles of Each Company of the Fourth, Twelfth, Twenty-First and Forty-Fourth Georgia Regiments, with a Short Sketch of the Service of Each Member, and a Complete History of Each Regiment, by One of Its Own Members*. Atlanta, Ga: Franklin Print. And Pub. Co., 1903.

Wellman, Manly Wade. *The Story of Moore County: Two Centuries of a North Carolina Region*. Southern Pines, N.C.: Moore County Historical Association, 1974.

Wheelan, Joseph. *Bloody Spring: Forty Days That Sealed the Confederacy's Fate*. Boston: Da Capo Press, 2014.

Wiley, Bell Irvin. *The Life of Johnny Reb: The Common Soldier of the Confederacy*. Baton Rouge: Louisiana State University Press, 1943.

LETTERS/FAMILY BIBLE

Albright Family Bible (used for family tree) privately owned by Larry R. Yow and used with permission.

Bibliography

Albright, Henry Alexander letter to his parents, May 16, 1863. Privately owned by Larry R. Yow and used with permission.

Albright, Henry Alexander letter to his parents, May 6, 1864. Privately owned by Larry R. Yow and used with permission.

Yow, Matthew C. Yow letters to various family members, April 1862 until April 1864. Privately owned by Larry R. Yow and used with permission.

Index

4th Georgia Infantry, 19, 158n4
7th Wisconsin Infantry, 120, 122
15th North Carolina Infantry, xxi, 79 (chaplain)
27th North Carolina Infantry, xxi, 79 (chaplain), 116, 163n12
46th North Carolina Infantry, xxi, 79 (chaplain), 108
48th North Carolina Infantry, xviii-xix (organization), xxi (part of Cooke's brigade), 65 (officers), 118 (at Appomattox), 124 (flag)
56th North Carolina, xxii
African Americans (see Black Americans)
Alabama, xvi
Albright, Nancy Catharine (see Yow)
Albright, Elizabeth, 147
Albright, Elizabeth A. Ward, 147
Albright, Henry A., xvii, 12, 24, 37, 42, 56, 57, 83, 85, 87, 90, 104, 109, 147, 153n28, 154n9
Albright, John E., xvii, 12, 13, 24, 37, 42, 56, 57, 83, 85, 87, 90, 104, 109, 147, 154n10
Albright, Joseph, xv, 41-42 (letter to JA), 57, 73, 77-78, 81, 82, 86-88 (letter to JA), 90, 93, 94, 95, 99, 100-101 (letter to JA), 102, 103-105 (letter to JA), 107, 147, 148, 169n12
Albright, Joseph Gibbs, 147
Albright, Kizzie R., 147
Albright, Margaret E. Farrell, 147
Albright, Nancy E. Lawrence, 147
Albright, Nancy Whitsitt, xv, 147
Albright, William S., xvii, 44, 147, 162n22
Albright, Youtha Ann, 3, 102, 147, 169n16
Allen, Joseph P., 128
Allen, Raleigh S., 128
American Revolution, 100, 169n15
Anderson, Lt. John H., 19, 158n7
Anderson, Gen. Richard H., 109, 110, 171n8
Antietam, battle of, xx, 126, 153n21
Appomattox Court House, 118, 124, 127

Index

Arkansas, xvii
ars moriendi, 114
Ashe, Thomas S., 166n17
Baker, William H., 128
Ballard, William, 128
Barlow, Francis C., 110
Barnhart, Charles A., 128
Barr, Stephen M., 129
Beauregard, Gen. P. G. T., 116
Beck, Daniel, 129
Beck, George D., 129
Bible, 34, 50, 60, 100, 102, 114, 172n27
Big Bethel, battle of, xvii
Black Americans, 25 (free Blacks in Petersburg), 151n4 (slaves in Yow and Albright families), 159n21 (free Blacks in Petersburg), 173n39 (Colored troops at Battle of the Crater)
Black, Malcolm, 129
Black, Malcolm A., 129
Blandford Church Cemetery, 115, 119, 172n31
Bloody Angle, 111
Bloody 48th, xix
"Blue and the Gray, The", 120, 122-123, 174n5
Boone's Mill fight, 55, 164n19
bounty money, xviii, 5
Boydton Plank Road, 117
Brady, Isaac, 19, 129, 158n5
Brady, Wesley W., 129
bread riots, 76, 165n3
Bridges, Horace A., 129
Bristoe Station, battle of, xxiii, 74, 85, 87, 127
Britt, Joseph, 129
Broadway, Andrew A., 129
Broadway, Samuel W., 129
Brower, Amelia Yow, 146
Brower, Wesley, 81
Brower, William N., 5, 37, 80, 85, 96, 97, 146
Brown, Jesse, 146, 174n3
Brown, Joshua, 147
Brown, Mary Elizabeth Yow, 146
Bryant, Kelly, 130

Index

Buffalo Church, xviii
Burnside, Gen. Ambrose E., xxi, 173n39
Camp Mangum, xviii, xix, 1, 4, 5, 6, 118, 124, 154n6
Campbell, Alexander, 128, 130
Campbell, George B., 38, 130, 161n9
casualty statistics for 48th NC, Co. D, 125-127
Chaplains, 79
Christian brigade meetings, 34, 79, 165n8
Christian, Sam, 81, 166n17
Clegg, Capt. Thomas J., 5, 6, 19, 22, 155n12, 158n12
Clegg, Lt. Montraville D., 104, 170n20
Clouts, Alex A., 130
Coggin, Zack, 130
Collins, William A., 157n34, 159n23
Cold Harbor, battle of, 116
Confederate Congress, xviii, 154n7, 166n17
Confederate Dead, 115, 119
Confederate Postal Department, 3
Confederate States of America, xvii
Conscription, 4
Conscription Act of 1862, xviii
Cooke, Gen. John Rogers, xxi, xxii, xxiii, xxiv, 37, 51, 87 (injured at Bristoe Station), 93, 105, 108, 116, 117, 160n5, 163n12, 167n24, 167n32, 167n34, 167n35, 169n19
Cooke, Gen. Phillip St. George, 93
Cox, Hugh B., 130
Cox, Miss, 25, 159n20
Crater, battle of the, 116-117, 173n39
Craven, Solomon, 130
Craven, Thomas G., 83, 147, 167n21
Craven, Mary Eleanor Albright, 147
Crisco, John, 98, 168n7
Crotts, Amos, 130
Crotts, Andrew C., 130
Crotts, George, 131
Crotts, William, 131
Crouch, Augustine, 98, 168n8
Daniel, book of, 58
Davis, Baxter, 131
Davis, Charles, 131

Davis, Enoch, 131
Davis, Henry, 131
Davis, Jefferson, 60, 63, 165n29
Davis, Raleigh, 131
Deaton, Burwell, 131
Deaton, John M., 131
"Dead March", 111
Deep River Mining and Transportation Co., 151n3
desertion, 47-49
Dodson, Rev. Charles C., 79, 166n12
Dorcas (See Dorcas S. Maness Yow)
Dorsett, Samuel J., 131
Dorsett, William Wesley, 132
draft (see conscription)
Dowd, Captain James C., 22, 26, 27, 28, 29, 35, 37, 158n13
Du Pont, Rear Adm. Samuel F., 162n21
Dunker Church, xx
Early, Gen. Jubal A., 110
Ellis, John W., xvii, 153n24
Eppes, Doctor, 157n31
Evans, Henry, 132
Ewell, Gen. Richard S., 108, 111, 153n31
Fairley, Rev. David S., 79, 166n10
fasting, humiliation, and prayer, days of, 59-60, 101, 165n29
Fields, Henry A., 132
Fields, Joseph H., 132
Finch, Francis Miles, 120, 123
Fine, Gabriel, 132
Fine, Jonathan S., 132
Five Forks, battle of, 117
Florida, xvi
Forrest, James, 132
Fort Stedman, battle of, 117
Fort Sumter, xvii, 42, 162n21
Foster, Gen. John G., 164n19
Fredericksburg, battle of, xxi, 159n26
Freeman, Isaac, 132
Freeman, James A., 132
Freeman, John W., 133
French leave, 161n13

Index

French's Farm, battle of, xix, 19, 20, 21-22, 124, 152n18, 159n22
Gallimore, M. C., 133
Gallimore, William, 133
Garner, Monroe, 39, 161n12
Georgia, xvi
Georgians, 19
Gettysburg, battle of, xxiii, 48, 94, 163n11, 163n12, 163n14, 167n33
Gilmore, William, 133
Globe Tavern, battle of, 117
Good Death, the, 114, 172n30
Graham's Battery, 87, 167n29
Grandfather (See Andrew Yow)
Grant, Gen. Ulysses S., xxiv, 107, 108, 110, 111, 112, 116, 117, 118, 170n2, 172n32
Green, G. W., 133
Gum Swamp, battle of, xxii
Hall, Col. Edward D., 87, 167n35
Hancock, Reuben, 133
Hanover Junction, 112, 127, 171n19
Harper's Ferry, xx
Harrington, John M., 133
Harrison, A. T., 146
Harrison, Christopher Columbus, 14, 89, 97, 99, 102, 157n33, 167n36, 169n17
Harrison, Lydia A. Yow, 146
Hatcher's Run, battle of, 117
Hayes, James W., 148
Hayes, Mary Jane Yow, xv, xvi, 18, 56, 59, 66, 148, 151n5
Hearn, Solomon S., 133
Hendley, Calvin, 133
Heroes of America, 159n27
Heth, Gen. Henry, xxiii, 87, 109, 112, 116, 167n33
Hewlett's Station, 112
Hill, Gen. Ambrose Powell, xxiii, 108, 109, 110, 112, 118, 122, 153n31, 167n33, 170n6, 171n18
Hill, Gen. Daniel H., xxii
Hill, Col. Robert C., xix, 4, 20, 37, 38, 124, 152n13, 158n10
Hoke, Gen. Robert F., 167n23
Holcombe's Legion, 53, 163n14
Holden, William W., 81, 94
"Home Sweet Home", 111

Index

Horner, 86, 167n26
Howerton, Rev. Samuel W., 79, 166n11
Hudson, John, 133
Huger, Gen. Benjamin, xix
Hunsucker, James M., 96, 133, 168n3
Huntley, Stephen, 134
Huske, Maj. Benjamin R., xix, 12, 19, 152n15, 157n32, 158n8
inflation, 75-77
Inverted V design, 115, 121, 172n32
Iron Brigade, the, 122
Isaiah, book of, 58
Jackson, Samuel, 134
Jackson, Stonewall, xx, 153n31
James River, xix, 12-13 and 15 (battle on JR)
Jericho Mills, battle of, 112, 120, 122, 123
Johnson, Brantley Benjamin, 134
Johnson, Duncan M., 134
Johnston, Gen. Joseph E., 152n18
Jones, Nancy Elizabeth (see Yow)
Jones, William Hogan, 65
Kessley, John H., 134
Key, Rials, 134
King's School House (see French's Farm, battle of)
Kirkland, Gen. William W., xxiv, 105, 108, 167n30, 167n32
Lambeth, James H., 134
Lawhon, Cornelius D., 113, 134, 153n23, 172n22
Lawhon, Capt. William H. H., 65, 113, 116, 128, 157n31, 171n21, 172n27, 173n36
Lawhon's Crowd, 61
Leach, Neill, 134
Lee, Gen. Robert E., xxiii, xiv, 73, 100, 107, 108, 109, 110, 112, 115, 116, 117, 118, 121, 127, 152n18, 163n12, 169n13, 170n6, 172n32
Lewis, James H., 135
Lewis, W. G., 135
Lincoln, Abraham, xvi, xvii, 117
Longstreet, Gen. James, xxi, 108, 109, 110, 166n14, 170n6, 171n8
Louisiana, xvi
Maddox, George W., 135
Malone, Benjamin, 136
Manassas, first battle of, xvii

Index

Manassas, second battle of, xx, 26
Maness, Henry, 53, 163n14
Maness, John Lewis, 37, 44, 102, 146, 160n6
Maness, Julia A. Yow, 146
Maness, Lewis G., 23, 24, 25, 54, 159n15
Maness, Reuben, 60, 97, 98, 165n30
Mangum, Peter J., 136
Marye's Heights, xxi
Maryland Campaign, xx
Mason, xvi
Mathis, Malphus, 136
May, Joseph J., 136
May, Thomas A., 136
McClellan, Gen. George B., xix
McLean, Allen C., 135
McLean, Archibald, 135
McNeill, Hector, 135
McNeill, Noah, 135
McPhail, M. J., 135
McRae, Daniel R., 135
Meade, Gen. George G., xxiii, xxiv, xxv, 108
Melton, George W., 136
Memorial Day, 123
Miller, B. F., 136
Mine Run Campaign, xxiv
Mississippi, xvi
Moffitt, Mr., 78, 83, 97, 165n7
Moody, Peter, 9
Moore, George, 92, 168n41
Moore, J. W. E., 136
Morgan, Edward D., 136
Morgan, James G., 37, 38, 136, 161n7
Morgan, Nathaniel, 137
Morris, Daniel, 137
Mount Olivet Lodge, No. 195, 113
Mule Shoe, 111
Myers, Jefferson C., 137
naming patterns, 18
"Nearer, My God, to Thee", 111
Negros (see Black Americans)

Index

Norfolk and Petersburg Railroad, xix, 9
North Anna Battlefield Park, 120-123
North Anna River, battle of, 115, 172n32
Oath of Allegiance, 100, 169n12
Overland Campaign, 106 (map), 110-116, 127
outliers, 2, 154n1
Parish, Jesse B., 137
Parish, Thomas, 137
Paschal, David C., 137
Paschal, Nathan, 137
Peace Movement, 94
Peninsula Campaign, xix
Phillips, Baxter C., 137
Phillips, Ed, 137
Phillips, Eli, 137
Phillips, Martin C., 138
Phillips, Stephen, 138
Phillips, William L., 138
Plyler, Rev. Calvin, 79, 166n13
Po River, battle of, 110
politics, 93-95
Pool, Mrs., 95, 96, 98
Pool, William, 7, 11, 138, 155n20
Porter, Horace, 110
Quakers, xvi
Randolph, George W., 47
Ransom, Gen. Matt, 164n19
Ransom, General Robert, xix, xxi, 10, 12, 20, 21, 152n17, 158n9
Reams Station, battle of, 117
Rice, Robert, 138
Rich, Anthony T., 147
Rich, E., 138
Rich, Jane Albright, 147
Rich, John N., 83, 147, 166n20
Richardson, David, 138
Richardson, Enoch, 138
Richardson, John C., 138
Riddle, James, 138
rings, carved, 3, 45, 56, 69, 163n8
Roberson, Henry, 138

Index

Robbins, NC, xv
Robinson, Col. William W., 122
Rodgers, Abner, 139
Rouse, Enoch, 139
Sanders, Simon, 139
Saunders Field, 110
Seagroves, James, 139
scarlet fever, 166n14
secession, xvi, xvii, 152n8
Seven Days Battles, xix, 19-20
Seven Pines, battle of, 152n18, 163n7
Sharpsburg, battle of (see Antietam)
Shaw, Unknown, 86, 167n27
Shaw, Dr., 98, 167n27, 169n9
Sheridan, Gen. Philip H., 117
Sherman, General William T., 117
Shiloh Church Cemetery, 144, 149
Short, Burwell H., 139
Shortell, Cpl. Michael, 120, 122, 123
Sinclair, Daniel F., 139
Sinclair, Daniel M., 139
Slavery (see Black Americans)
Smallpox, 2, 40, 41, 162n17
Smith, Elias, 139
Smith, Gen. Martin L., 172n32
Smith, Thomas, 139
South Carolina, xvi
South Side Railroad, 117
Southern Express Company, 168n6
Spear, Col. Samuel P., 164n19
Spence, Henry A., 139
Spotsylvania Court House, battle of, 110-111
Stedman, William A., 139
Stewart, Enoch, 140
Stewart, Robert B., 140
Stewart, Samuel D., 24, 140, 159n18
Stuart, Flora, 93
Stuart, Gen. James Ewell Brown 'Jeb', 93
Stutts, Andrew J., 7, 11, 19, 22, 50, 140, 156n21
Stutts, Cornelius A., 56, 68, 69, 140, 164n22

Index

Stutts, G. L. M., 140
Stutts, George D., 140
Stutts, Henry W., 40, 41, 50, 140, 161n14, 162n17
Stutts, John H., 36, 40, 41, 77, 78, 79, 99, 103, 140, 156n21, 160n4, 161n14
Stutts, Sarah E. Yow (Matthew's aunt), 156n21
Stutts, William C., 140
substitution, 4
Sullivan, Franklin, 141
Sullivan, Isaac McLendon, 141
Swicegood, Henry F., 141
Taylor, C. T., 141
Taylor, D. W., 141
Teague, W. B., 141
Ten Percent Plan, 169n12
Tennessee, xvii
Texas, xvi
Texas Brigade, 109
Thompson, Lt. John A., 65
Traveller, 109
Vance, Zebulon B., xxi, 47, 49, 94, 104, 105, 153n24, 160n28, 167n23, 167n30, 169n15, 169n19
Vicksburg, 48, 49, 94
Virginia, xvii
Virginia Central Railroad, 112, 115
Virginians, 25
Waddell, J. M., 108
Wadford, E. F., 141
Wainwright, Col. Charles S., 112
Walker, Gen. John G., xix, xx, xxi, 20, 21, 22, 158n9
Walkup, Col. Samuel H., xix, xxi, 47, 65, 113, 116, 117, 152n14, 156n26, 157n34, 160n28, 163n8, 163n9, 167n30
Wallace, Calvin, 141
Wallace, Eli, 141
Wallace, John M., 141
Ward, Lawrence M., 147, 174n4
Ward, W. S., 142
Ward, W. W., 142
Ward, Rachel D. Albright, 147
Warren, Gen. Gouverneur K., 112, 122
West, Alexander, 142

Index

Wilcox, Gen. Cadmus M., 112
Wilderness, battle of, 108-110
Williams, Isaac, 24
Williams, George W., 142
Williams, Harbert, 142
Williams, John P., 142
Williams, Jonathan J., 142
Williamson, Dave, 54, 164n17
Williamson, Hy, 54, 80, 83
Williamson, John, 21, 43, 92, 158n11, 168n42
Williamson, Mrs., 43
Williamson, Wiat, 57, 164n23
Willis Hill, xxi
Wilmington and Weldon Railroad, 164n19
Winchester, Lt. John R., 65
Wood, James, 142
Wright, James, 82
Wright, Levi, 82, 84, 85, 86, 142, 166n18, 167n28
Yellow fever, xx, 26
yeoman, xvi
Young, H. S., 142
Yow, Ada J. Brown, 148
Yow, Andrew (grandfather), 14, 23, 30, 52, 57, 84, 157n35
Yow, Andrew C., 142
Yow, David D., 3, 7, 9, 45, 143, 156n22, 156n24
Yow, Dorcas S. Maness, 96, 146, 168n4
Yow, Elizabeth, 146
Yow, Elizabeth R. Maness, 40, 53, 99, 154n5
Yow, Henry, xv, 4 (letter to HY), 23, 28, 29, 30, 44, 52, 54, 61, 80, 83, 84, 85, 91, 101, 146, 151n4, 154n5
Yow, Isaac, xxiii, 5, 7, 11, 21, 24, 40, 45, 50, 52, 56, 57, 59, 79, 83, 85, 87, 91, 98, 103, 146, 155n14, 155n19, 159n19, 162n25, 163n10, 168n4
Yow, John Matthew, xxii, 18 (birth and naming pattern), 28 (name confirmed), 148-149 (occupation, marriage, death)
Yow, Joseph Gibbs, xv (birth), xvi, xxii, 18 (naming pattern), 45 (cap from Papa), 97 (wants Papy to come home), 98 (wants to sit in Papy's lap), 148-149 (occupation, marriage, death)
Yow, Leola A. King, 148
Yow, Mariah E. Craven, 148
Yow, Martha J. Garner, 146

Index

Yow, Mary Elizabeth Harrison, 146

Yow, Mary Jane (see Mary Jane Yow Hayes)

Yow, Matthew Christenberry, xv (birth, marriage), xvi (Mason and farmer), xviii (enlisted CSA), xx (ill- yellow fever), xxii (furlough), xxiii (injured at Bristoe Station), 64 (image), 112 (mortally wounded), 143, 146, 148, 153n23

Yow, Nancy Catharine Albright, ii (frontispiece image), xv (parents and marriage), 18 (gave birth), 146-147 (family trees), 148-149 (life after Matthew died and her death)

Yow, Nancy Elizabeth, xv (birth), xvi, 3 (ring received), 18 (naming pattern), 56 (ring mailed to her), 59 (letter to NEY), 66 (image of letter to NEY), 69 (image of ring), 148-149 (life as adult and death)

Yow, Nancy Elizabeth Jones, xv, 146, 151n1, 154n5

Yow, Nancy Harrison, 14

Yow, Rebecca, 146

Yow, Sarah, 91, 146

Yow, Simeon Jones, xviii, xxiii, 5, 6, 7, 8, 10, 11, 15, 17, 20, 21, 22, 24, 37, 40, 45, 50, 52, 56, 57, 59, 79, 82, 83, 85, 86, 87, 88, 90, 91, 98, 101, 102, 103, 146, 155n14, 155n17, 159n19, 162n25, 163n10

Yow, William, 143

Yow, William A., 146

Yow, William Henry, xv (birth), xvi, 18 (naming pattern), 58 (eats peaches), 58-59 (letter to WHY), 67 (image of letter), 148-149 (occupation, marriage, and death)

www.ingramcontent.com/pod-product-compliance
Lightning Source LLC
Chambersburg PA
CBHW021309060526
44119CB00101B/408/J